Meraki Journey

Transitioning from a Liability to an Asset for Your Purpose

Dr. Christina Baker

Copyright © 2022 Dr. Christina Baker

All rights reserved.

ISBN: 9798877923201

DEDICATION

This book is dedicated to each beautiful soul who has nurtured, encouraged, motivated, and inspired me to become the woman that I am today. In this lifetime, I call you friends, but you are more like angels, wrapped flawlessly in beautiful skin. Keep being the trailblazers, the nurturers, the true embodiments of royalty, the nonjudgmental ears, the reason for belly cramping laughs, and the tissue box holders during tearful moments. You are a flashlight throughout my darkest days, and an encourager on days when I feel like giving up. You have been the voice of reason during my lowest moments, celebrated me during my highest moments, and motivated me during the moments in between. And more importantly, you have empowered me to continue to foster the strength, and courage to face my reality with tenacity, power, and grace. My humble prayer, and desire is to return the favor by influencing as many people to strive to become better versions of themselves, as you are still doing for me each day. Because of you, I have the audacity to wake up each morning, ready to be the best version of myself, both for myself and for everyone that I'm assigned to cross paths with during my lifetime. Forever grateful, forever inspired, and forever your loyal friend. Thank you.

-Dr. Christina A. Baker

MERAKI'S TABLE OF CONTENTS

Acknowledgments	i
Black Queen by McTerry Obioha	1
Part 1: Recognizing Your Liabilities Through Self-Awareness And Healing	3
Part 2: Transitioning From A Liability Through Self-Love	61
Part 3: Becoming An Asset Through Self-Care	85
Part 4: Maintaining Through Self-Check-Ins	100
Conclusion	114
Dear GOD by Jesmine Shelton	117
Author's Message	118

ACKNOWLEDGMENTS

Black Women:

Today, I salute you and acknowledge the countless sacrifices that you make for love and progression. Your noticed and unnoticed sacrifices are equally beautiful, and I appreciate you for them. I want to take this opportunity to thank you for all the times that you have been a shoulder to cry on, and for remaining resilient throughout uncomfortable moments. I am honored to have this platform to acknowledge you, because your beauty is my beauty, your cry is my cry, and your history is mine. So, I don't need to know your name, your current situation, nor your life story to know that you possess infinite power to own your own path, and walk it with grace, confidence, and strength.

You symbolize the kind of hope that activates the pulsing desire to strive for greatness. Though you may not always feel like hero you are each day, you are never alone. Somewhere out there, there is another queen fighting the same fight, but may be waiting on your survival and testimonies to pull her through. Because of you, and the queens who precedes you, I give you your flowers in honor of the empowerment that you have influenced. I need you to know that I see you, I am proud of you, and I am rooting for you. Never forget that the true essence of royalty trails behind you, causing heads to turn and minds to wonder, "Who is she?" And I will never be surprised that, she is you.

Black Queen by McTerry Obioha

This poem is dedicated to all the beautiful black queens of the groundbreaking past, the innovative present, and the promising future.

Black queen, often criticized

And stigmatized for the gifts

You were born with, that others visualize.

In a world of doppelgängers,

Your radiance stands alone

Setting the tone for others to try

To duplicate and re-create.

The crown which you possess

Will always remain after

Centuries of progress and regress.

Black queen, don't fall victim

To the fiends with constant lust dreams.

Your journey, none like no other,

For one day may you give birth

To a generation of future kings and queens

With qualities of their mother.

Black queen, learn to feel and heal

From life's pitching of ordeals.

For the love you give holds great power

And is unique. Not one for a coward or the weak

Black queen, black queen, may your distinct glow

Gleam and you reign supreme.

-McTerry Obioha

Part 1: Recognizing Your Liabilities Through Self-Awareness And Healing

     Meraki Journey combined with the Meraki Journal creates a healing and self-transformational process of reshaping your mind and behavior, to better align with your goals and desires. So, before getting started, please feel free to purchase the Meraki Journal, for note taking and to participate in various types of self-help activities, that supports the topics of this book. This journey will equip you to take back your power, by not allowing negative experiences and past traumas to write your story for you. From start to finish, Meraki Journey will break down processes of recognizing and correcting your liabilities, becoming an asset for your purpose, and elevating yourself and others through self-awareness, self-love, and self-care.
     No matter your age, race, gender, or socioeconomic status, we all have traits that may hinder us from accessing our full potential in specific areas of our lives. However, it takes a wise and brave individual to recognize their liabilities, and take the necessary steps in rectifying them. So, whatever your reason for joining me on this journey, I am honored, and extremely proud of you. I commend you for your commitment to wanting to become better versions of yourself daily. Throughout this experience, please keep in mind that nothing worth having will ever happen overnight, nor will it happen in a straight line.
     Some days, you may want to give up. Some days, you may feel like your transformation is no longer worth pursuing. Some days, you may feel stagnant, or feel like you're taking multiple steps backwards. And, some days, you may feel like you're strong enough, and motivated enough to conquer anything that life throws your way. However, on each of those days, always remember your *why*, and never give up on yourself. This is a friendly reminder that your intentionality, determination, and

willingness to become better versions of yourself, each step of the way is required of you. However, also keep in mind that taking mental, physical, and emotional breaks, until you're well enough to continue is equally essential.

Meraki Note: *The best way to know if you need to push through, or take a wellness break from something, is through self-awareness.*

For the entirety of this process, always remember to be patient with yourself, and know that you are worth all of the benefits that comes with becoming an asset.

1.A Self-Awareness

Self-awareness is about taking the time to mentally and emotionally be present in everything that you do.

      Self-awareness is the recognition and understanding of your actions, feelings, biases, triggers, preferences, and insecurities. In simpler terms, to be self-aware is to know yourself on a deep and intimate level. However, because we have gotten so used to hearing that self-awareness is important, we have subconsciously dismissed the validity of it all together. Yes, it is essential to know yourself on the deepest levels, but why? Why is self-awareness so important? Oftentimes, when we know the reasons or the effects of our decisions, we are more likely to put our all into achieving the best outcomes. Because, knowing our *why* makes the decision more personal, rather than doing something simply out of duty.

Our Why: Self-awareness is a crucial first step in any self-transformational journey, because it influences wisdom, understanding, and discernment during internal and external experiences. Allowing you to decipher between what is moral vs. immoral, and what is ethical vs. unethical. As opposed to making sound decisions with only relying on the simple surface of what is right vs. wrong.

Self-awareness is responsible for high-level decision-making skills, like:

1. Knowing the difference between needing a break from something versus having the pressing urge to procrastinate.
2. Knowing the difference between declining an invitation out of wisdom versus declining an invitation out of fear, hate, or bias.
3. Knowing the difference between having a discerning spirit versus having the spirit of paranoia due to past hurts and traumas.

Self-awareness is also a gracious form of self-love because it gives you the gift of knowing where you are in life. Knowing where you are in life emotionally, spiritually, and mentally is a great first step before creating a plan on how to get to your desired self. This concept is similar to that of a GPS. A GPS must first pinpoint your current location, or your desired starting point, in order to effectively give directions to a specific location. This is a key reason why self-awareness is the initial step in the Meraki Journey of self-transformation and healing.

Two main ways of becoming self-aware:

1. Slow down and pay close attention to how you operate during specific situations, such as:
    a. High-Level stressful experiences
    b. Working under pressure
    c. Completing time sensitive tasks

  d. Dealing with difficult family members, friends, coworkers, etc.

  For example, when paying closer attention to our reactions and habits in specific situations, we may notice that we tend to lash out on others during high-level stressful experiences. Or we may notice that we experience severe anxiety when dealing with time sensitive tasks, causing us to procrastinate or to perform poorly. Sometimes we get so caught up in how life is affecting us, that we forget to analyze how our reactions are affecting our environment, and the lives of others. Becoming aware of our reactions to specific people or things can lead to creating new boundaries, lowering or raising our tolerance levels, becoming intentional about our self-control and discipline, and becoming more intuitive.

 2. Pay close attention to how you react to others whenever you are experiencing a specific mood, feeling, or emotion, such as being:
  a. Tired
  b. Frustrated
  c. Depressed
  d. Happy
  e. Overwhelmed
  f. Accomplished, etc.

  For example, we may realize that we overextend ourselves to others when we are in a good mood. Or that we tend withdraw ourselves from others when we are feeling sad or frustrated. Both reactions can be liabilities. Overextending ourselves will cause us to eventually give from an empty cup; leaving us with less than enough to take care of our own mental, physical, or spiritual wellbeing.

  Likewise, using isolation as a coping mechanism

when depressed or overwhelmed, is just as damaging. It is essential to know that, when we are at our lowest, that's when we will need our most trusted, and loved village to pour into us the most. Please keep in mind that isolation cuts off our supply of love, support, encouragement, and resources. Becoming aware of actions that are tied to our emotions is important when seeking to master logical and rational decision-making, and to become a more stable thinker.

Meraki Note: *Self-awareness makes it much easier to notice which behavior is working to your detriment, and which adds value to you. In other words, simply slowing down and practicing self-attention will influence you to realize which behavior needs to be changed, and which needs to be increased, in order to create a better environment for you and those around you.*

Take Away Point: *Self-awareness is necessary in:*

- *Formulating reasons for change*
- *Becoming a stable thinker*
- *Cultivating wisdom, and high-level decision-making skills*

Self-Awareness: Traits

No individual is ever all good or all bad. Each of us have our own biases, triggers, and tolerance levels. These components are all a part of what makes us so unique. However, _how they affect_ our behaviors, morals, and thought process is what causes us to perform as a liability or an asset in life. Therefore, it is important to always be aware that:

- Our biases can contribute to stereotyping, and unfair treatments of others.
- Our triggers can directly or indirectly affect our healing process.
- Our tolerance levels can affect our ability to set healthy boundaries.

Exercise found in the Meraki Journal: *Using your triggers to pinpoint areas of your life that needs healing.*

1.B   Trauma Triggers & Authentic Healing

A trauma trigger is a stimulus in the mind that causes involuntary recalls of unpleasant or traumatic past experiences. This stimulus can be caused by a random thought, or environmental elements, such as a scent, a song, a show, the presence of a specific person, or your current situation. Trauma triggers are oftentimes inevitable, and can affect your mood without warning. Therefore, taking the time to become more self-aware will allow you the intimacy of recognizing what your triggers are. This action is the starting point to disarming the effects of your triggers.

Our Why: Once you are healed from the pain that is attached to unpleasant memories, inevitable trauma triggers will become ineffective to your mood and behavior.

Meraki Note: *Triggers are like potholes in your journey, depending on the size of it, it can either slow you down, or cause new damages. Therefore, it is important to become aware of your triggers, and rectify them in the early stages of your journey, to avoid creating new traumas that you will later need to heal from.*

On another note, please take comfort in knowing that, it isn't uncommon to feel traumatized, hurt, or triggered by something, without knowing where those emotions are actually stemming from. So, in your Meraki Journal, you will be prompted on how to initiate specific healing, by using what was meant to cause further harm— *aka: your triggers.*

<u>Meraki Note:</u> *Please be advised that not all activities that are included in your Meraki Journal will be found in this book.*

<u>In Your Meraki Journal:</u>
1. Write down 1 or more of your triggers. For example:
    a. A specific type of scene in a movie
    b. All new forms of rejection by a job, loved ones, school, etc.
2. Write down the unpleasant memories that each trigger brings to mind. *If possible, please take this time to write in specific details.*
3. Write down 1 or more reasons why each memory is unpleasant for you. For example:
    a. Experience of physical, emotional, spiritual, or financial damages
    b. Emotions you've experienced during the time of the event
    c. Specific details of what happened to you in that moment
4. Explain the (current) mood or emotions that you experience when this memory is triggered? Ex: anger, sadness, embarrassment, defeat, loneliness, violation, regret, etc.
5. Explain how you've dealt or coped with this trigger prior to today. Ex: self-isolation, lashing out on

others, explosive outbursts, abusive eating, self-medicating, and/or extreme intoxication.
6. In specific details, write down what you believe would make this memory a little less painful or uncomfortable. Ex: forgiveness, new boundaries, justice, and/or specific changes.
7. Ask yourself "is this solution reasonable, moral, ethical, and/or attainable?" *If the answer to this question is no, take some time to figure out what you may need to change or transform within yourself in order to arrive at a better solution.*
   ***The goal of trying to arrive at a better solution isn't to lie to yourself or sugar coat your feelings. The goal for this section is take the power away from your traumas or negative experiences. When we disarm traumatic experiences from negatively influencing our thoughts and behaviors, we will regain control of our feelings, perceptions, thought process, and actions.**
8. Once you've decided on a good solution, the next step is to create a plan of how to achieve it. In your journal, write down at least the first 3 steps of your thoughted out plan. *Please note that each trauma or negative experience may require very different action plans.*

<u>Meraki Note:</u> *Though you may already know the answers or responses to each prompt, writing it all out in your journal will relieve your mind from the duty of safeguarding such heavy thoughts. It will also help you to better make sense of how, and what you've been feeling since the traumatic event took place. Therefore, please don't do yourself a disservice by not fully committing to tasks that are meant for the betterment of you.*

Authentic Healing & Forgiveness

Healing is the path to inner peace, confidence, strength, and happiness.

     For the most part, when on the topic of healing, our minds may quickly refer to a time when someone has wronged us in a very hurtful or traumatic way. However, healing doesn't always have to be about what others have done to us. Sometimes, healing is about forgiving ourselves for how we have treated ourselves in the past. Dealing with the hurt of terrible decisions and poor self-treatment—especially due to ignorance and older traumas. Which can cause a massive amount shame and regret. But I want you to know that you are worthy of forgiveness and grace for every self-inflicted hurt—whether they were intentional or not. Instead of demonizing or punishing yourself for all the discomfort that you have caused, it is more beneficial and productive to learn from the mistakes you've made, and use those lessons to fuel your growth, wisdom, and maturity.
     Forgiving others, and achieving healing from what others have done to you is never easy, but I believe that once you have gotten pass self-forgiveness, you will be stronger and more equipped to genuinely set yourself free from the bondages that unforgiveness imposes onto you. Please know that it is not silly, or weird to give yourself a sincere apology, and take the time that you need in order to sincerely forgive yourself. Oftentimes, we've heard the saying, "love starts at home: you must first love yourself, in order to love others correctly." This concept is parallel to healing and forgiveness. Let your experience of forgiving yourself guide you through the process of forgiving others.

HEALING & SELF-TRANSFORMATION

Meraki Note: *Healing from self-inflicted hurt and hurt inflicted by others are both equally important to address. So, for the remaining of this section, we are addressing both types of hurt and trauma.*

Forgiveness

I believe that unforgiveness is one of the greatest liabilities, because it has the power to change who you are at your core. It controls the way you love, your perceptions, your emotions, your interaction with others, and it also burns hate into your heart. I understand that forgiveness may seem like an unfair thing to do, because you may feel like you're letting your offender off the hook way too easily. And sometimes, forgiveness may feel like self-betrayal, or a betrayal of a loved one; especially if the hurt is still present.

Forgiveness isn't the stamp of approval to get over the pain and trauma caused by an experience. It's okay to forgive someone while still trying to heal from the effects of your hurt. Never rush or minimize your pain in an attempt to convince yourself that you've legitimately forgiven someone. Yes, it is possible to fully forgive someone, while still struggling with the issues that their actions have caused you or your loved ones. Always keep in mind that your trauma, your pain, your grief, nor your hurt has an expiration date. So, take your time and give yourself permission to feel the emotions that you are feeling; even after you've forgiven your offender.

There's another saying that goes: forgiveness is not for the offender, it's for the forgiver. However, although this saying is very true, it is easily dismissed; especially when you are so influenced and driven by your pain. When we are deeply submerged into our pain, oftentimes, we couldn't care less if forgiveness is for the other person or not. I believe that this staying is mainly agreed upon, or realized after true forgiveness has already been accomplished. However, this saying isn't very helpful to our emotions, while in the midst of struggling to forgive. So, let's try something new. Whenever you're experiencing difficulties with forgiveness, try to remind yourself that *"Forgiveness isn't a door to dismiss your pain, nor to dismiss the accountability of your offender. Forgiveness is the key to removing the shackles that will keep you bound to your pain forever"* –Dr. Baker (2022).

Meraki Note: *Trying to heal without forgiveness is like trying to heal with bullet fragments still inside your body. Yes, there's a possibility that you will survive, and live what seems to be a regular life. But you will never be fully healed. Authentic healing requires genuine forgiveness. Which equates to locating, and extracting all bullet fragments from your wound. So that once you are healed, there are no probabilities of later complications occurring from the old trauma.*

Triggers When Healing

There is nothing wrong with wanting to stay away from triggers, until you're strong enough to withstand the pressures that comes with it.

During the healing process of a physical wound, it is essential to keep that area away from all items that may cause an infection or increase the pain. You would treat the wounded area with a little more care and love until it's healed enough to withstand normal or increased pressure. Because in the beginning of the healing process, this area may be the weakest and most sensitive. We all know that it is wise to keep elements like rubbing alcohol away from a cut, to avoid stinging pains during the earlier stages of the healing process. However, once the wound has dried up, those elements will no longer affect the area where the wound once was.

This understanding should also extend to your spiritual, mental, and emotional healing. In many aspects, healing from a psychological or emotional wound should be dealt with the same courtesy and tediousness as a physical wound. When trying to heal from traumas, you may experience extreme vulnerability and impressionability. Therefore, despite what others may believe about your decisions, it is important to stay clear of people, places, and things that negatively impact your healing process. But like a physical wound, remind yourself that staying away from specific people, places, or things isn't a permanent exercise in your healing and self-transformational journey. In other words, the things that used to trigger unpleasant memories, induce negative emotions, or disrupt your healing process, will no longer have the power or the accessibility to affect you in the end.

Always remember that authentic healing is about trusting the process, being intentional about who and what has access to you, and staying aware of your triggers. Staying away from triggers while healing, allows you to create physical and mental sacred spaces for your healing, and peace of mind to safely progress.

Four Tiers Of Authentic Healing

1. *Inner peace*
2. *Confidence*
3. *Strength*
4. *Happiness*

Meraki Note: *Before we get into the four tiers of authentic healing, let's address the popular saying, "hurting people, hurt people". The true statement is <u>unhealed people hurt people</u>. No matter how badly hurt we've been, once we* *have healed, matured, and learn from our pain, our desire will be to see others healed as well.*

1. Creating Your Sacred Space And Maintaining A Positive Presence During Your Healing

Tier 1 is all about cultivating and maintaining inner peace. Peace is one of the most essential elements for the improvement and maintenance of self. Much like how the body needs a safe place to rest and sleep in order to perform at its best each day; peace is what the mind yearns for when it needs to unwind, recuperate, heal, and/or mature. Creating a sacred space and maintaining a positive energy is the way to create and maintain inner peace.

Sacred Spaces: Your safe space is also known as your sacred space. A sacred space is where you go to feel the most comfortable, safe, free, secured, and protected. Therefore, for most of us, our homes would be an ideal sacred space. However, this is not the case for everyone, so we will discuss physical and mental sacred spaces. A sacred space can be a prayer room, your mind, your entire home, your car, your journal, or even a specific area at your favorite park. A sacred space allows you the freedom and privacy to do whatever that gives you peace.

Your mental and physical sacred spaces should reflect how you feel about yourself, what you accept for yourself, and what you want for yourself. It should emulate the respect, and love you have nurtured within self. Your sacred space should have a kind of atmosphere that influences humbleness and quietness within you, to sit and evaluate mistakes made. In addition to influencing you to learn life lesson from those mistakes.

Sacred spaces are beneficial when trying to get through any unresolved feelings, or issues that you may have. In doing so, you are able to think more clearly, uninfluenced, and without judgmental opinions from others. Consistently visiting your sacred space is the key to mastering the art of trusting your own judgments and starving self-doubt.

Meraki Note: *No matter where your sacred space is, always remember that it should provide a clean and control environment for your unmasking and raw healing.*

Meraki Journey's Self-Check: *Every now and then, ask yourself a series of questions, that will aid you in creating and maintaining a healthy sacred space. A few ideal questions are:*

- *Do I feel safe to express myself freely in this space?*
- *How do I feel mentally and emotionally when I enter this space?*
- *Do I feel physically and spiritually safe here?*
- *What movies, music, or media am I using to feed my mind in this space?*
- *What foods and drinks have I been indulging in that aren't good for me—causing me to feel sluggish, unmotivated, and unhealthy?*
- *What art, furniture, or other items do I still have in this space, that triggers negative thoughts, memories, and/or behaviors?*
- *Am I my most authentic self in this space?*

Remember to always answer these questions with complete honesty. Your honest answers to these questions will aid you in adjusting or changing anything that is negatively feeding your mind, body, spirit, and emotions in the sacred space that you are creating.

To those who don't have the luxury of being in control of the dynamics of your home or any other physical spaces, please know that there are other ways of creating a healthy sacred space. If not equally important, creating a mental sacred space is especially important. Because, if you don't have a peace of mind, it is highly unlikely that you will ever feel at peace in any physical location.

Creating a Mental Sacred Space:

1. Journal Entries
    a. Feed your mind with positive and kind words
    b. Write out future plans
    c. Complete written activities that will aid you in your healing process
    d. On days when you are feeling overwhelmed: Document your feelings, to relieve your mind from all that you have kept bottled up over the span of days, weeks, or longer
2. Take walks to clear your mind or to check-in with self
    - Remember that healing doesn't happen in a straight line. So, be consistent with self-check-ins to make sure that you are still on the right path.
3. Create a mood board to document your dreams, desires, goals, resolutions, and accomplishments.
4. Free-write about how you feel, whether in journal form, poems, music, or story form (using real or fictional names and events).
5. Read books or listen to podcasts that positively impact your mind and heart
6. Reread old journal entries, stories, or poems whenever you feel overwhelmed, triggered, or unmotivated, to:
    a. Recenter your thoughts

b. Reignite your motivation and determination to continue your healing process

<u>Meraki Note:</u> *As much as you can, be mindful of the videos or shows you watch, the types of books you read, the types of conversations you engage in, and the type of music you listen to.*

The best way to be mindful of these things is to ask yourself:

- *How does this type of music, show, or book make me feel?*
- *How do I feel after having a specific type of conversation?*
- *Does it promote motivation, peace, inspiration, kindness, or love?*

<u>2. Realizing And Rectifying Your Faux Healing: Band-Aids</u>

The process of true healing isn't easy by any means. It is an uncomfortable and tedious process. Tier 2 is all about having the confidence in knowing that you don't have to cover up your scars, in order to seem more appeasing to others; or to make others feel more comfortable in your presence. Self-confidence isn't always about being vibrant and center staged. It's the exercise of humility, and having the ability to be compassionate, patient, and understanding in the most uncomfortable situations. I encourage you to be confident enough to deal with your healing authentically. Never try to mask the pain of your traumas by pretending to be okay on days when you aren't.

Please keep in mind that just because your hurt subsides occasionally, doesn't mean that your wound isn't still there. Temporary moments of happiness, or having a good day doesn't equate to being healed. In those moments, it is very likely that your pain is dormant, waiting to flare up in dangerous ways when triggered. Being mindful of your triggers is very important. However, realizing and rectifying your habits of masking your hurt, or pretending to be okay when you aren't, is the best way to minimize unexpected depressive episodes, or traumatic lash outs.

Ways of band-aiding your pain:

- Distractions
    - Always wanting to be around others
    - Endless scrolling on social media
    - Binge watching shows, movies, and videos
- Substance abuse and/or overeating
- Avid love-seeking
    - The irrational desires of needing to feel loved by anyone
    - The hunger to always feel recognized, validated, or rewarded
    - The deep crave for praise in professional, social, and/or private settings
- Temporary happiness
    - Shopping
    - Vacations or Getaways
    - Partying, etc.

Consequences of faux healing: Much like a physical wound, if left uncared for, your emotional wound will get infected. Which is the festering and growth of anger, hate, depression, resentment, sadness, and insecurities. These types of emotions will spread by first affecting the areas closest to it. In other words, your lack of healing will eventually affect the people closest to you; by you spewing out harmful words, toxic behaviors, and spreading negative energy. Not only will you affect others, your anger, depression, and insecurities will spread internally by affecting your mental and physical health. Therefore, it's safe to say that pretending to be healed from your traumas will cause more strain on your personal life, than the temporary uncomfortability of going through your healing process.

New Identity Through Healing

Please find solace in knowing that not all wounds lead to scars. Yes, it is possible to heal from something without having any residue lingering over you. Yes, you can come out as a completely different individual than you once were. Many times, we may find ourselves feeling the pressure to still enjoy the same things that we once did. Or to operate in certain situations the same way as the unhealed versions of ourselves did. But I would like for you to know that you don't need to feel guilty for not being the person that you use to be before your healing.

Maybe before your healing, you were the life of the party, the wild child, the most outgoing individual, and masking every pain with a smile and a good time. But now that you have gone through your healing, you may feel more confident by being reserved, observant, and intimate. Because of this, you may experience loved ones and acquaintances alike, expressing that you're no longer fun to be around. Or they may use the word *"change"* in a negative way. Please don't let that discourage you from maintaining your healing.

Stay true to who you're most comfortable as. Because, no matter what, you will always encounter people who will judge you for changing. They will judge you for no longer liking the same things, or no longer speaking and behaving in the same way. They will even be disappointed that you are no longer their source of entertainment. But you will also encounter others who will celebrate you for growing. They will be inspired by all that you have overcome, and all that you have gained. So, choose your support system wisely.

__Meraki Note:__ Disclaimer: there's absolutely nothing wrong with being the life of the party; in the same way that, there's absolutely nothing wrong with being a more reserved individual. However, there will always be something wrong with you not being your authentic self, just to please others. Each stage of your life may require a different version of you. So, never feel that staying the same is an act of loyalty. Rather, it is an act of self-sabotage. Therefore, let's agree that the ultimate goal should always be to grow, elevate, and evolve.

__3. Dismantling Your Survival Mode To Experience Authentic Healing__

When you take the time to become more self-aware, you may realize undesirable behaviors that may have once seemed normal to you. This may be because your actions and reactions were filtered through your survival mode. Survival mode is a defense mechanism that you consciously or subconsciously develop during or after a traumatic event. We do this because we believe that these new traits will protect us from further hurt. Tier 3 is all about the strength that it takes to break out of traits, and habits that have been our norm for so long. In other words, it takes an immense amount of strength to not be "stuck in your ways" anymore.

As humans, whenever we get hurt—whether it was traumatic or not—our heart and mind is affected the most. So, we build a fort around them, to avoid ever getting hurt again. *This is the epidemy of a survival mode.* I believe that the span between experiencing hurt and starting the journey of healing, is when survival modes may be acceptable. However, to successfully complete your healing and self-transformational journey, you are required to strip down the armor, in order to heal what you've been shielding all this time.

      Moreover, we may use anger or self-isolation to keep others away from what we are protecting. But as uncomfortable as it may feel at first, true healing can only happen if we are brave and strong enough to expose the parts of us that actually needs the healing. But keep in mind that dismantling your survival mode doesn't mean that you forget the lessons that your trauma, and other experiences has taught you. Healing and self-transformation is about knowing that you're not meant to be closed off from the rest of the world. You just need to give access only to who, and what is conducive to your health and quality of life.

Meraki Note: *In order to heal, you have to be willing to let go of the patterns and traits that you developed while enduring your traumas. Remember that who you had to become when you were in your survival mode, isn't who you need to be today.*

4. Pursuing Vs. Cultivating Happiness

      The last tier of Meraki Journey's Healing is authentic happiness. Sometimes, the pursuit of happiness isn't the same as cultivating happiness. Chasing happiness is almost always contingent on the object or person that you are seeking happiness through. Once that thing or person is no longer in your life or is temporarily unavailable, your happiness becomes absent. However, when you focus on being a happy person in spite of external factors, that's when you are truly able to shift your perspective, and see goodness in more than what meets the eye. Learn how to cultivate happiness instead of pursuing happiness.

Pursuing: To pursue is to go after or chase something or someone. In other words, no matter how hard you try, you will always be behind what you are pursuing. True happiness should come from within. Therefore, how can you chase something that is already a part of your being? Oftentimes, we may hear statements like, *"I'll be happy when I have a couple thousand dollars in my bank account."* Let's take a moment to think? Does this statement mean that, if this goal is never accomplished, you'll never be happy? And if this goal is accomplished, do you sincerely believe that you will then experience true happiness, or will you set out to achieve a new goal to sustain your happiness?

Meraki Note: *The first question implies that your happiness in contingent on something that may or may not happened, or last over a span of time. The second question implies an endless pursuit of happiness.*

The pursuit of happiness is almost always contingent on external factors like people, fame, money, materialistic things, etc. This is not to say that you shouldn't be excited about materialistic things. This is to say that external elements should be a bonus to your happiness, and not the source of it.

Cultivating: To cultivate is to develop or nurture something. Cultivating happiness is the reliance on internal factors to be happy; like self-love, self-care, finding your purpose, accomplishing personal goals, and feeling at peace. But know that cultivating happiness doesn't numb you from feeling or getting hurt. It teaches you how to deal with your hurt in a healthy way. It also teaches you how to love yourself through the pain, instead of destroying yourself because of your pain.

1.C Tolerance Level and Setting Boundaries

A tolerance level is the peak of your ability or willingness to endure or have the patience for something or someone. Keep in mind that because we are complex and diverse human beings, our tolerance levels will not be the same across the board. In other words, sometimes, a healthy level of tolerance for one situation, may not be a healthy level for another. Knowing where your tolerance levels are for specific situations, will allow you to decide whether you'll need to adjust such levels to better align with your goals or purpose.

Why is monitoring your tolerance level so important?

Having a low tolerance level for someone, will mainly affect *your* behavior. While having a high tolerance level for someone will increase your acceptance of *their* behavior. Self-awareness will allow you to discern which situation requires a higher or lower tolerance level, in order to produce the most beneficial outcomes.

<u>*Meraki Journal Exercise:*</u> Becoming aware of your tolerance levels can be a good starting point for creating healthy boundaries. The exercise in the Meraki Journal will assist you on setting healthy boundaries, and maintaining a beneficial tolerance level for various types of experiences and relationships.

Setting Healthy Boundaries

Give yourself the space to heal, limit triggers, and cultivate peace.
      Setting boundaries can sometimes feel cringy and daunting; causing us to feel as though we are betraying or abandoning those who we care about and love. But I want you to know that having boundaries is not the absence of care or concern for others' feelings, wants, or needs. Healthy boundaries are more of an exercise of having discipline, intentionality, a healthy balance, and mutual respect. These types of exercises will allow you to discern when it is important to preserve someone's feelings, and when their hurt feelings are due to the lack of healthy boundaries.

Setting healthy boundaries includes:

- Speaking up for yourself in situations
- Exercising discipline
- Saying no to things that does not serve your wellbeing
- Sticking to your set boundaries

      Healthy boundaries are necessary in order to have healthy platonic, romantic, familial, and professional relationships. This is the best way to set standards that will help you in balancing various aspects of your life. Remember that boundaries aren't meant to offend, or to please anyone. It is to safeguard your peace, goals, and priorities.

Meraki Note: *Sometimes, feeling emotionally and mentally overwhelmed and exhausted may be influenced by the lack of healthy boundaries. It is very likely that you are emptying your cup for others, because you aren't* *comfortable with saying no. Nor have the discipline to take on things in moderation. Sometimes, even after we allow others to max us out, we then allow ourselves to go into overdraft. This is one of the main reasons why setting healthy boundaries is essential in protecting our mental, spiritual, emotional, and physical health.*

Self-Discipline By Living A Fasted Lifestyle

One trait that will make setting boundaries easier is self-discipline. And the most effective way to strengthen your self-discipline is through fasting. Fasting is formally known as a voluntary abstinence from food and drink for a specific purpose and length of time. Which is why the first meal after a long period of not eating was known as *breakfast*. The purpose for fasting usually involves health, ceremonial, ethical, or religious reasons. However, the Meraki Journey of self-transformation defines fasting as, the abstinence from *anything* for a certain amount of time, for your overall wellbeing. This type of discipline gives you the steady control to influence your behaviors and thoughts in positive ways.

When living a fasted lifestyle, fasting isn't viewed as a last resort solution, or a method for damage control. With consistency, an individual who is living a fasted life will occasionally fast from:

- Social media
- Family, friends, and/or acquaintances
- Addictive activities
- Addictive foods
- Negative influences

When you are fasting from these things, you are not only doing it to avoid becoming too attached or addicted to it. Fasting allows you to put that time and effort into something more beneficial and productive. Give yourself the chance to learn what your true desires and needs are. Take these moments to learn what you truly love to do, what music you love to listen to, and what activities you like to do, without worrying if it is socially acceptable or not. Learn about yourself, learn a new craft, learn something that will help your business, learn something that your future self will appreciate you for. Fasting gives you the space, and foundation to invest into yourself, and your future.

<u>Meraki Note:</u> *A fasted lifestyle will help you to avoid becoming consumed by negative people, trends, and other negative elements. Which may stunt your growth, leave you stagnant, provoke triggers, and/or cause darkened emotions.*

**Fasting increases discipline, and discipline makes setting boundaries easier.

<u>*Saying No And Exercising Intentionality*</u>

In the words of Pastor Touré Roberts, your *no* is important, because your *yes* is very expensive. The cost of your yes is your time, your energy, your money, and your availability. So, be intentional about what you say yes to, and also be intentional about what you're saying no to. Feeling obligated to people please, or feeling guilty at the thought of saying no to a request, can cause extreme anxiety, and even resentment. This is why saying no to things that doesn't serve your wellbeing, goes hand-in-hand with setting boundaries.

Struggling to say no to things that doesn't serve you, shouldn't have anything to do with the other person. Saying no to things should have everything to do with how you treat yourself. It is better to choose yourself, your wellbeing, and your quality of life over disappointing others. On the other hand, in the spirit of having a balanced life, please know that there's nothing wrong with changing your plans every once in a while, to accommodate others. But refrain from making a habit out of being okay with putting yourself on the back burner for the sake of others' feelings.

Meraki Note: *It's okay to be unavailable, even if you didn't previously have your own plans. It's okay to say no to connections, friendships, and relationships that doesn't serve you anymore. And it's okay to respond to text messages, without feeling pressured to return phone calls. Having healthy boundaries is about choosing not to pressure yourself in doing anything that will jeopardize your sanity, healing, or safety.*

1.D Liability Categories

Each liability is an opportunity for change, and a starting point for progression.

The three groups of liabilities that Meraki Journey focuses on are cultural liabilities, personal liabilities, and generational liabilities.

Our why: Familiarizing ourselves with the three groups of liabilities is important, because it gives light to where our traits and behaviors stems from, and also where they lead to.

Biases → Encourages Stereotypes → Causes Cultural Liabilities → Creates More Biases

Triggers → Affects the Healing Process → Causes Generational Liabilities → Creates More Triggers

Tolerance Levels → Affects Setting Boundaries →

Causes Personal Liabilities → Influences Other Tolerance Levels

**Please keep in mind that some liabilities can be categorized in more than one group.

1. Cultural liabilities are negative traits noticed in people who share specific cultural identities.

*<u>**Meraki Note:**</u> There are 10 known cultural identities, which can be recognized by using the acronym <u>ADDRESSING</u> (Hays, 2008). Your cultural identities are your **A**ge/generation, **D**isability (developed), **D**isability (acquired), **R**eligion/spirituality, **E**thnic/racial identity, **S**ocioeconomic status, **S**exual orientation, **I**ndigenous heritage, **N**ationality, and **G**ender.*

One universal cultural liability is the unfair perception of men who express their feelings—especially if done so publicly. Self-expression is beautiful, liberating, and brave for any gender. However, we have gotten so accustomed to what society deems to be the appropriate actions or reactions of a man. These cultural expectations are liabilities because it stifles the voices of men, which causes resentment, bottled up emotions, or liable outbursts. I genuinely believe that it is unfair and immoral to expect anyone to appreciate, and value something that they themselves are deprived of. In other words, we shouldn't expect a man to appreciate or value women expressing themselves, if he hasn't experienced the beauty and liberation that comes with the freedom to express himself.

As a woman, feeling safe, secured, and protected by any man that I associate myself with is very important to me. Therefore, it is my duty to be someone who gives men the feeling of security, protection, and safety to freely express their feelings. Let's create a culture where gender equality isn't only fought for in career compensation or job opportunities. We must also strive for mental and emotional gender equality.

Meraki Note 1: *Commonsense is to know that equal does not mean identical.*

Biases: *Men expressing their emotions* → **Stereotypes:** *Men are feminine or weak if they express their feelings* → **Cultural Liabilities:** *Toxic masculinity.*

Dear Black Men,

It is high time that we experience the serenity of a wholesome mental and emotional health. No longer will our actions be dictated by passed transgressions, our communities, nor our history. We don't need to bottle up our emotions, or put on a brave face when times are hard. Rather, find solace in the fact that having a clear mind, and heart will not only influence us to be better men, but great ones. Always remember that you can achieve true happiness through having open communications with loved ones, work through uncomfortable emotions, and sometimes just simply letting go. Let's make it our new normal to have level-headed conversations throughout disagreements, instead of yelling or shutting completely. Make it a habit to listen to the other side, and express your thoughts and feelings regarding the problem; in hopes of arriving at a mutual understanding.

Admitting when we're wrong isn't common in our culture, but we need to become aware of when our ego is working at our detriment. Our egos may help with sports and our careers, but may affect how we communicate; causing a simple conversation to turn into an argument or misunderstanding. Instead of adamantly defending your wrong doings, it is more honorable to respect yourself and others, by taking responsibility for your actions, and doing better in the future. Starting now, we will love and give intrinsically. Therefore, any act not reciprocated in our favor will not lead to negative reactions nor bruised egos. Rather, we will simply gain happiness from our actions.

It is important to know that sometimes letting people and things go is essential for our emotional and mental health. For example, you may have been hurt by an ex-partner in the pass, which, unfortunately, is affecting the way you treat your current partner, or even the way you now perceive relationships. So, I am encouraging you to become aware of the liabilities, that you may gain through remaining emotionally connected to individuals, who are nothing but poison to the elevated version of you. It is time that we no longer allow anyone to dictate our personality and life choices. I encourage you to learn how to fully love yourself enough to choose peace, love, and unity. Over hate, strife, and toxicity. Lastly, though we may want to be there for the ones who we care about, please know that it is important for us to take care of ourselves first, so that we can better take care of others.

A less serious cultural liability is the "fashionably late" trend. To me, this is a liability because I believe that punctuality speaks to the level of our discipline, and the respect that we have for others, and our own time. Many have glorified the culture of lateness by cosigning statements like, "people who are always late live longer." It amazes me to see how quickly a liable mindset that encourages toxic behavior, procrastination, and limited thinking are normalized; especially when commercialized by celebrities. This is the epidemy of a cultural liability.

As a group, let's become more respectful of time,

and responsible enough to plan ahead. Let's unnormalize behaviors that supports stereotypes, that influences us to not be taken seriously as a group. And let's give back commonsense its power, by knowing that planning ahead increases the chances of punctuality, while decreasing the chances of stress or potential injury caused by rushing. Instead of glorifying, or cosigning negative traits, let's invest our energy into traits that supports a more elevated version of ourselves.

Meraki Note: *Your behavior does not have to align with, or be similar to the majority, whether you identify with that specific culture or not.*

2. Personal liabilities are habits or personality traits that no longer aligns with the person you desire to be.

Self-victimization is a powerful personal liability to our purpose. Sometimes, we may view our circumstances as personal attacks. Which will affect the way that we choose to deal the problem. If we flood our minds with the thought that God is punishing us with our life experiences, our minds will be robbed of the capacity, to realize that our experiences are not personal attacks. Our experiences are simply preparing us to be well equipped, to successfully execute our purpose. When we self-victimize, or foster the feeling of being under attack, our defense is to resist the process that bends us into the right shape for the job.

Meraki Note: *Resisting growth will only anchor you to the problem.*

Yes, we all have a purpose, but each time that we refuse to submit to life's lessons, we are delaying our progress. The heat of our circumstances may cause us to become soft temporarily, but it gives us the flexibility needed to bend, and take on the shape best suited for who we're meant to become—Dr. Baker (2022). Remember that life is about learning, elevating, and evolving. So, trust that the lessons you've learn in one season of your life, will become your greatest assets in the seasons thereafter.

Meraki Note: *Our low tolerance for a specific problem can cause us to disregard healthy boundaries. In other words, sometimes when trying to escape from our problems, we may settle for hanging out with misaligned company, or engaging in activities that are not aligned with our life's assignments. Which is a personal liability.*

Low **Tolerance Levels** of our problems → Unhealthy **Boundaries** with others → **Personal Liabilities** of delaying multiple types of elevation.

Meraki Exercise: If you struggle with this type of self-victimization, please complete the activity in the Meraki Journal.

Though self-victimization is a liability from the start, keep in mind that there are other personality traits that may have started out as an asset to your purpose, but later became a liability. For example, being an empath in one chapter of your life, may have helped you to have compassion, and become more mindful of others' feelings. However, in another chapter of your life, being an empath may have caused you to overextend yourself for others. Which then affected the way that you showed up for yourself each day. Self-awareness will allow you to know which traits has expired in your new season, and are ineffective for future positive outcomes.

Meraki Note: *Growth is when you are able to change your method, after realizing that an old way of doing things is now fruitless for current situations. Changing fruitless methods by:*

- *Dismantling survival mode traits*
- *Staying out of your own way, by not being 'stuck in your ways'*
- *Gaining wisdom through life's lessons.*

**In addition to wisdom, and discernment, self-awareness influences growth.

3. Generational liabilities are familial habits or behaviors that does not align with God's purpose for your life. <u>Generational patterns aren't always the guideline for your life. Please know that it's okay to choose your own path if need be.</u>

Meraki Note: *Although this is a generational liability, it is a personal recognition. Meaning, what may be a liability to the success of your purpose, may not be a liability to the success of a relative's purpose. Therefore, I encourage you to never demonize or force anyone to identify a behavior or habit as a liability; just because it is a liability for <u>your</u> progression. Please remember that your journey is customized to you, and no one else.*

The most talked about generational liability is generational curses. However, there are many other types of generational liabilities, such as negative learned behaviors, unresolved emotions, and negative perceptions. Another example of a generational liability is the "strong black woman" stigma or mindset. For centuries, there has been limitations, and higher expectations of black women, than any other group of people. Which has shown up in the ways that we have been taught to deal with our emotions, how to be independent and fierce, and how to never let our guards down in any situation. Because unfortunately, we are the least protected group of people in this world.

Dear Black women,

I admire how well you carry yourself, even on days when you would much rather be carried. However, let's learn that being strong doesn't equate to accepting unnecessary behaviors, enduring negative treatment, or taking on more than you should handle at a time. Be intentional about giving yourself some grace, and know that you are doing the best that you can. Never allow anyone to weigh in on what your best should look like, and never allow anyone to define what strength means to you. Please find comfort in knowing that your best may not produce what others have. But stay the course, and focus on your own life's journey, and what's meant for you will get to you right on time.

I want you to know that it's okay to not be the strong one, who always has it all together. It's okay to not want to figure everything out all on your own. And it's okay to not care about "defying all odds" every day. Not because you have the ability to handle a lot at once, doesn't mean that you should. I encourage you to be your own definition of strength. Be vulnerable if you want to. Lean on your support system if you want to. Have a good cry whenever you want to. And leave somethings for another day if you want to.

Give yourself permission to simply be who you are. You are delicate, you are nurturing, you are comforting, you are graceful, you are sweet, and you are mind-

blowingly beautiful, both inside and out. Remember to always be kind to yourself, and learn how to put some things down for a moment. It's okay to want to prioritize that business that you've been meaning to start. It's okay to put yourself first for a moment after having a long week at work. And yes, your kids are your responsibility, but it's okay to ask for help, while trying to manage other responsibilities. Yes, you are well capable of standing alone, but even an island needs the support of the ocean. Surround yourself with people who keeps you afloat, and adds value to you. You are not a strong black woman. You are strong. You are black. And you are a woman.

-Christina Baker

<u>Meraki Note:</u> *Triggers of past experiences may cause us to fall back into our survival mode. Which may ultimately cause us to display the "Strong black woman" mindset, or the strong man who keeps everything to himself. This type of behavior will delay our progression and healing process. And when we aren't healed, we will unknowingly pass on toxic behaviors to our children and dependents.*

Triggers → Affects the Healing Process → Causes Generational Liabilities

<u>How to become aware of a liability?</u>
If a behavior, mentality, or trait is strong enough to cripple you in at least one of the five elements of your being, which are your perceptions, thoughts, feelings, words, and actions, it is a liability.

Example 1: <u>Unforgiveness</u> can affect how you <u>feel</u> around the person that has wronged you, and it can also affect your <u>perception</u> of that person, or their cultural group. In other words, because of unforgiveness, you may develop a bias against a specific cultural group—gender, race, religion, etc.

Example 2: Though procrastination may not affect your feelings, it affects your actions. Meaning, you can be very motivated to complete a task, but low discipline may cause you to put that tasks off for another day. Your lack of discipline will develop personal liabilities, which may influence unhealthy boundaries.

<u>Meraki Note:</u> In most cases, one liability will produce or fuel another; causing a snowball effect of issues. Therefore, it is wise to rectify a liable trait in its early stages, by using the method of change or transformation.

Change Vs. Transformation

What are the differences between change and transformation?

Whether cultural, personal, or generational, our liabilities are oftentimes habits that we cling to, in order to pacify the effects of our less-than-ideal past experiences. Though our hurt may have been out of our control, we have allowed the effects to form who we are today. This is why change and transformation are crucial steps in the healing process.

The effects of our traumas can cause us to:

- Be impatient
- Suffer with depression
- Participate in addictive behaviors
- Be involved in trauma bonding relationships (platonic and/or romantic)
- Love without healthy boundaries

- Be stubbornly unforgiving

<u>Change:</u>

As said by Palinkas (2021), change is a substitution of the norm in response to *external* factors. External factors are experiences that happens *to* us, and around us. Which means that change is influenced by factors that are outside of self. For example, rules at work, relationships, and cultural trends are all things that are happening around us or to us—as opposed to within us. Positive self-transformation will always require healthy changes. Hence, making changes in your personal life should cater to the success of your future. So, keep in mind that your reason for change should not align with a culture that goes against becoming an asset to your purpose; nor should it be about the desire to please others.

Here are the four main guidelines that Meraki Journey uses to lessen the chances of making changes to please others, or to contribute to negative cultures:

1. Decrease unlimited access to yourself from negative or misaligned individuals by:
    - Cleaning up and monitoring your inner circle
    - Becoming intentional about the content that you read, watch, and listen to
    - Avoid environments that are consumed with rage, hate, violence, and other negative energies
    - Being mindful of the type of conversations that you indulge in by,
        - Engaging in conversations that are positively stimulating

- Staying away from conversations that does not serve your healing and self-transformational desires.
  - *Such conversations include putting others down, and negative self-talk.*
2. Monitoring your behavior on social media by:
   - Being mindful of the type of content that you share
   - Being mindful of the type of content that you expose yourself to
   - Avoid comparing yourself to others
3. Eliminate unhealthy competition with others
   - Remember that life is about learning, elevating, and evolving through self-awareness, self-love, and self-care.
   - Celebrate others' successes, no matter where you are in your life; and know that someone else's success should not represent the absence of yours.
   - Always keep in mind that, though you may crave for someone else's fruits, you will never truly know the full story of their roots. So, clap for others, while focusing on developing your own story.
4. Disregard cultural timelines of:
   - Marriage
   - Starting a family
   - Finishing school
   - Starting a career, etc.

All due respect to the many variations of cultures, beliefs, and religions. However, when it's all said and done, cultural timelines are man-made—which, each has its own pros and cons. Change and transformation is about your personal beliefs and choices, as opposed to cultural beliefs, and opinions. This is the most authentic way to live a peaceful and happy life.

Meraki Note 1: *Change is a bit more sophisticated than we give it credit for. For example, change is neither a positive nor negative decision.*

Question: What can cause a change to be a positive or negative decision?

Answer: 1. The outcome or reason behind the change. 2. Your intentions, mood, and emotions that precedes the change.

Meraki Note 2: *Always remember that it is your responsibility to make sure that your intentions for change is not fuel by the opinions of others, cultural trends, or comparing your life to the life of others.*

Transformation:

Transformation is a fundamental *internal* evolution in our beliefs (Palinkas, 2021). Internal evolutions are the experiences that happens *within* us, as opposed to what happens *to*, and around us. This means that transformation is influenced by shifts in our perspectives of others, our past experiences, and current situations. Transformation is also influenced by the development of our own beliefs, whether it be religious, spiritual, political, ethical, or moral. Our beliefs can be influenced by books, religion, music, influencers, and the company that we keep. Though books, religion, music, etc., are all external factors, it is our beliefs, thoughts, feelings, and perceptions of the external factors that influences our transformation.

Question: If external factors influence change, and our beliefs in the external factor influences transformation, why isn't change and transformation the same thing?

Answer: Though intertwined, they are different. Your beliefs aren't required in order to make a change. However, transformation depends on what we truly believe.

For example, an individual can make changes due to peer pressure, laws, or the fear of seeming different, without believing in anything that supports any of their changes. However, please keep in mind that the longer you practice a changed behavior, the more it becomes a part of who you are. In other words, although change and transformation are different, they oftentimes influence the outcome of each other.

Meraki Note: *When you lower the chances of making changes that are influenced by external factors, you are simultaneously lessening the chances of transforming due to tainted or toxic beliefs.*

Methods of distinguishing between change and transformation:

1. When making a change in your life, you are essentially replacing a specific trait for another. Hence, something about you will be <u>different</u> in the end.

A changed person: An individual can change from always arriving to work late, to becoming a punctual person. This isn't due to any inner conviction. Rather, this change may be due to the fear of being subjected to dire consequences.

2. Transformation consists of developing, and maturing a trait, which will cause the trait to become <u>more efficient,</u> as opposed to different.

A better giver: An individual can transition from being a selfless giver, to being a wise giver. Hence, positive self-transformation is about becoming a *better* version of yourself. Which, in some cases you may seem like you are a completely different person. However, all that you desire to become is already within you. The process of self-transformation is simply what you use to access it.

Meraki Note: *Self-awareness will gift you the knowledge of knowing which liability needs to be changed, and which needs to be transformed.*

1.E Shifted Perspectives

You cannot solve a problem with the same thinking that created it.
-Albert Einstein

Our Why: A shifted perspective is a great way to initiate specific healing processes. Many of us have been taught that we are all a result of our past experiences. However, though this statement may be true, I believe that <u>how we perceive</u> our past experiences is what influences us to become a liability or an asset to ourselves. Shifting your perspective is a vital way to strip your childhood trauma of all the negative influences it may have on your behavior as an adult.

Self-Awareness → Change or Transformation → Shifted Perspective → ← Healing

Meraki Note: *As mentioned above, a shifted perspective can initiate your healing process; in the same way, your healing can also initiate a shift in how you perceive other experiences.*

Self-Check-In Question: Is my perspective causing me to behave as a liability, or an asset to my goals, aspirations, purpose, or livelihood?

Hero Or Villain?

The interpretation of how we perceive our traumas can make the difference between whether we are casted as the hero or villain in our own stories. In other words, are you a liability or asset to your purpose?

    Let's take a brief look at a supervillain and a superhero who both experienced similar childhood traumas, but opposing adulthoods. Maleficent grew up as an orphan after the death of her parents, where she then thought that she was the only one left of her kind. Like Maleficent, Supergirl also thought that she was the only one left of her kind, after her planet was destroyed. And was also under the impression that both of her parents had died. Both powerful women have very similar backgrounds. However, the main difference between them was their perception of their traumas. Causing one to become the villain in her story, and the other became the hero of hers. Therefore, is it safe to say that authentic healing, and true forgiveness, are all great tools to grant positive perception; in hopes of creating a better reality for ourselves. I believe that there is power in our perception because it has the ability to disarm the long-lasting effects of our traumas.

The Zoom-Out Method:

Meraki Motto: *See yourself as a whole, rather than a zoomed in version of yourself.*

      Meraki Journey has created The Zoom-Out Method to aid in shifting your perspective of your past experiences. This method encourages readers to take ownership of their whole reality, as opposed to just snippets of their lives. This method will also allow readers to practice various ways to initiate their healing process, and unconditional self-love.
      Being fixated on negative past experiences may influence us to only see ourselves as unworthy of anything better. When this is the case, we are more likely to stay zoomed in on our downfalls, failures, insecurities, and imperfections. Which may result in us cropping out parts of ourselves that proofs worthiness of abundant love.
      The longer we keep our minds zoomed in on a particular area of our lives, the more we will believe that that version is the full view of who we are. But always remind yourself that, you are not defined by the things that you go through in life. You are defined by the choices that you make. And your choices are influenced by how you perceive your past and present experiences.

Method Description: *The Zoom-Out Method is completed in three separate phases. Phase 1 focuses on resolving the negative experiences that you've zoomed in on. Phase 2 focuses on shifting negative perspective of your experiences to a more positive one. Or to at least help you to see yourself in full view, rather than a partial view. And phase 3 focuses on changing and transforming personal qualities to make your life view better.*

Phase 1: Own it and Conquer it

1. In your journal, write out an experience that you've been zoomed-in on. For example: a hurt that you are struggling to get over. Or a mistake that you've made in the past, that is affecting your life currently.
   a. When writing, be detailed, be intentional, and be 100% truthful about the event.
   b. Then, in full details, describe how the experience made you feel at the time when it took place.
   c. Now, describe how the memory of this experience triggers you to feel now

Chances are you may never be able to shift your perspective, if you don't first try to figure out what is keeping you zoomed in on this specific experience. Use this exercise to learn what this experience is meant to teach you, in order to move on.

Meraki Note: *Life is about learning and elevating. So, please don't stay comfortable with the thought that good and bad things happens "just because".*

2. Read everything that you have written down twice
   a. The first time that you read this journal entry, is to make sure that you haven't left anything out. It will also give you the opportunity to add anything else that you would like to say.
   b. The second time that you read this entry, must be in the voice of your younger self.
      i. *The age that you were when the event took place*

ii. *This is the act of giving your younger self the voice s(he) may have never had.*

Apart from perspectives, internalized pain can dictate how our lives will turn out. Sometimes, we can have similar or identical experiences, but somehow our lives may still turn out to be very different from each other. This can be because one may internalize their pain. While the other may have had ways to express themselves, or had someone in their corner to help navigate their feelings. This exercise is to give your inner child, teenager, or younger adult self a chance to finally be heard. A chance to finally speak up for his/herself.

Meraki Note: *Your inner child is a reference to a younger version of yourself, who has not yet moved on from a specific aspect of your life.*

3. Write your younger self a letter
    a. Respond to what you believe your younger self was trying to express in the first letter
        i. Be attentive and caring
        ii. Avoid being dismissive of the pain that your younger self is expressing
        iii. Avoid being judgmental of his/her choices, and coping mechanisms.
    b. What is the most loving, heartfelt, and caring advice you can give your younger self?
    c. What helpful knowledge do you now have that you didn't have back then?
    d. Did your younger self go through that experience in vain, or are you using those life's lessons to make you and your younger self proud?

Meraki Note: *There's a strong possibility that you struggle to move on from this experience because you weren't heard, and you weren't helped. This is why, step 1 of The Zoom-Out Method is about giving your younger self a voice. And step 3 gives you the opportunity to be the adult that you wish you had when you were younger.*

Sometimes, the reason why your pain, regret, or disappointment may be screaming out so loud from within, is because that hurt inner child is not at peace with what has happened, or the decisions that you've made. Authentic healing is an act of self-love. You are gifting yourself with the priceless gift of peace—because you are worthy of it.

In an interview, Kevin Hart explained that, when you aren't able to heal, and move on from what has hurt you, you're stuck in that time period, forever. To me, this means that you are trapped in the mindset of your unhealed self. Causing permanent immaturity, until you successfully go through the process of healing and self-transformation. In other words, true maturity doesn't happen without proper healing.

Dear younger D. F.: *Instead of zooming in on the feeling of unworthiness because you were abandoned you as a child, and endured events that you are too scared and ashamed to talk about, zoom out and see all the elements that collectively make you who you are. When you zoom out, here's one of the many beautiful things that you will see: you will see a snippet of a day when you selflessly gave away your only umbrella to a mother and son, walking in the rain without any covering. Though that act of kindness may seem very insignificant to you, it may have been the one act of kindness that shifts their perspectives on a few things, or even influenced them to extend kindness to someone else. Your genuine selflessness is worth more than you can even fathom. How could you ever be unworthy* *when you possess the greatest gift, which is love. If only you knew how magical your love is! Please give yourself the opportunity to experience the magic of your own love.*

-Older D. F.

<u>Dear younger A. B.:</u> *When you zoom out, you'll see your goofy self and how much you make others laugh. Because of your goofy moments, you will have some of the best memories. Although I know that some of those moments were desperate attempts to shake your pain away. When you zoom out, you will give yourself the opportunity to focus on having more kind and goofy views of your life. Always remember that you are so much more than the things that you are currently focusing on. Please learn to zoom out, because it will save you from a lot of future self-sabotage, and a lot of unhealthy thinking.*

Sweet soul, you are not unworthy of love, you are a walking vessel of love. Never forget that failing at things is inevitable. So, why would life ever be measured by something that will happen regardless? But you know what's not inevitable? Getting up after a fall. Some of us will get back up swinging, and some will stay defeated. Getting up is a choice, and that is why your life isn't measured by failures, it's measured by what you choose to do with the inevitable.

Keep your head up! You're doing great! I love you.

-Older A. B.

<u>Meraki Note:</u> *The Zoom-Out Method gives you the power to make what once seemed to be the most hurtful and the biggest focus of your life, become small in comparison to the full scope of who you are. Shifting your perspective not only allows you to see yourself and your circumstances differently, it will help you to see others differently as well.*

Dear younger me,

With the utmost respect, I salute you for still trying to heal from things that you don't speak about. I sincerely hope that you heal from traumas that you never received an apology for, and traumas that may have been caused by your own lack of knowledge and guidance. You deserve the freedom, integrity, and confidence that comes with being healed—truly healed. Please don't fear the process of healing.

I wish I can hug you, and tell you that you will be ok. I wish I could comfort you on those days and nights when your brokenness would cripple you, to the point where getting out of bed felt impossible. I wish I could give you a spoiler alert, and tell you how happy and free you are now. Though I still have moments when memories of you breaks my heart, I wish I could tell you that you definitely cry less and less these days.

I know that working towards a place of complete healing can be messy, discouraging, and even cause you to relive some of your past hurts. But I want to let you know that it truly gets better, and you definitely get the hang of things more and more, with each experience. Thank you for the strength, and courage that you have displayed to get me to where I am today. I hope with all my heart that I'm doing you justice, and making you proud.

-Dr. Christina A. Baker

Phase 2: Positive Perspective

1. **Self-View:** In your journal, detailly describe your current self.
    a. Be honest. What do you say to, and about yourself on bad days—especially when no one is hearing you?

b. What are some good attributes that you have?
c. What is your favorite memory that involves your actions or words
d. What is your least favorite memory that involves your actions or words
e. Write down at least ten things that you love about yourself
    i. Speak *to* yourself as you would speak to someone who you love and *care* about
    ii. Speak *about* yourself as you would speak about someone who you love and *admire*

    Many of us may feel comfortable with giving others compliments, or even see the beauty in others. However, we may find it difficult or unnecessary to compliment ourselves. We may even find it difficult to see the beauty within ourselves without validations from others. And even then, we may still find it difficult to believe the positive words that others may say about us. Positive self-talk is crucial in your healing and self-transformational process. The goal is to get to a point where negative self-talk, and negative thoughts about yourself feels extremely uncomfortable for you.

    During phase 2 of this exercise, if you become aware of qualities that you may not like about yourself, the next step is to find positive, and beneficial ways to change or transform those qualities. Instead of beating yourself down, and criticizing yourself for every little thing. *You shouldn't tolerate verbal or emotional abuse from anyone, including yourself.*

Phase 3: Change and Transformation

Your past isn't going to change. It is cemented into your story. However, you have the power to change the that way you see yourself, and the that way you interpret your past experiences. This journal exercise is to help you to see yourself as a whole human being. It aims to give you the opportunity to highlight the good, the bad, the ugly, and the beauty of your life. As opposed to a zoomed in view of a specific, unpleasant area of your life.

After you have completed this journal entry, read out loud everything that you have written down so far. If your overall self-view doesn't sound like you're reading about someone you love, let's work on transforming your narrative.

On a new page: Based on what you have previously written, what are 3 things that you may need to change, and 3 things that you may need to transform?

Shifting Views:

1. Focus on celebrating your accomplishments: both big and small.
   a. Sometimes, you can be too focused on your failures, or what seem to be delayed success.
   b. Document all of your accomplishments, no matter how insignificant you may think they are. *Chances are your accomplishments may feel insignificant because you are comparing yourself to others. Or you may have people around you, who constantly downplay your achievements.*

**Always remember to be grateful for what you have, and where you are in life. While still doing your best to better yourself and your situation.

Meraki Note: *Flowers are never jealous of the sun's success because it doesn't need the sun to dim its light, in order to be the main focus of spring. In fact, flowers look their best when the sun is shining at its brightest. In other words, success should be the inspiration for others to also perform at their best. We should pride ourselves on raising each other up. Instead of comparing our worth and accomplishments to each other.*

2. Surround yourself with people who love, support, and adds to your happiness.

The trick to choosing your company wisely is self-love. Oftentimes, we surround ourselves with anyone just to avoid feeling lonely, fill a void, or because of the lack of self-love. But know that you are worthy of having kind, generous, loving, caring, and nurturing people in your life. I know that sometimes, these things are easier said than done. Maybe you don't trust to have *anyone* in your circle, because of past betrayal by those closest to you.

But please remember that the armor that you needed for survival in the past, may not be the same armor that you'll need moving forward. *T*rust that through gained wisdom, discernment, and understanding, you are now well equipped to choose your company wisely. Trust that you have grown mentally since your past experience. And trust that you have learned from your past experiences, instead of allowing those experiences to control your every decision.

3. *Make a conscious decision to live in a way that discredit the negative voices of your past experiences.*

<u>Manifesting a new Theme:</u> Have you ever felt like your life experiences had a pattern? A theme of bad things happening one after the other? Causing you to feel as though you are laced with a serious case of bad luck, or is stuck in the trap of multiple generational curses all at once?

I believe that healing from traumas, breaking generational curses, and shifting perspectives of yourself and your life all consist of manifestation. Changing and transforming the way we interpret our past will manifest a new theme for our lives. As mentioned before, we have control over five specific elements. Which are our perceptions, thoughts, feelings, words, and actions. Our perceptions, thoughts, and feelings are all taking place within us; and directly influencing our words and actions. While our words and actions are the two physical ways to manifest self into reality. These are the two bridges that directly connects self and the world. Which is known as *interaction*. Transforming self, and changing how we interact with others, is how we can manifest a new theme for our lives.

1.F Manifestation And Affirmation

Life is influenced by manifesting and affirming things, whether spoken out loud, written down, or whispered in your mind.

Have you ever experienced a slip of the tongue? Or have you ever said or done anything that you had no idea where it came from? This happens when what you've been feeding your mind becomes so cemented within you. So

much so, that it almost doesn't need your permission anymore to reveal itself. This is why it is important to feed yourself with things that influences you in positive ways. Intentional positivity is the key to reinforce kind words, thoughts, and actions within your daily life.
Here are some hacks to fostering positive thinking:

- Showing appreciation and gratitude for all that you have, and all of who you are
- State solutions, follow-up questions, or encouragements after stating a problem
- Find at least one positive thing in anything you go through in life.
- Engage in activities that induce positive thoughts by
  - Reading books that speaks to your intellect
  - Watching shows, movies, and videos that educates, inspires, and motivates you
  - Listening to music that affects your mind in positive ways
  - Engaging in healthy and positive conversations
- Use positive affirmations to replace negative thinking.

If it helps, create personalized affirmations to retrain your mind, to think a certain way. You can use the Meraki Journey's **P.O.W.E.R.** steps to formulate your own personalized affirmations.

1. **P**ride
    a. Name something about yourself or your life that you are proud of
2. **O**pportunities
    a. Be thankful for what you already have
    b. Be excited about what's to come
3. **W**isdom

       a. Name at least one thing that you have learned from any past experience
       b. What you intend to do with your new wisdom or knowledge
       c. What do you hope to learn in the future
4. Encouragement
       a. Speak positivity into your life, into your day, into your relationships, and into your craft. *(Anything that is connected to you, that you want to flourish).*
5. Royal Image
       a. Compliment yourself on at least one thing each day

An example of a full **P.O.W.E.R.** affirmation is 1. I am proud of the progress that I've been making—whether big or small. 2. I am excited about what my future has in store for me. 3. I will learn something new today that I will teach tomorrow. 4. I am destined for greatness. And 5. I am beautiful, both inside and out.

<u>*Meraki Note:*</u> *Never forget to speak life into yourself. Whether speaking within yourself or looking yourself in the mirror. Sometimes we would love for someone to speak kind words to us, acknowledge our efforts, and give us beautiful words of encouragement. Today, that person can be you. Tell yourself the kind and encouraging words you'd love to hear. Be your best and favorite cheerleader.*

<u>Affirmation Vs. Manifestation</u>

I would like to think that affirmations are helpful in building and maintaining our positive mindset. While manifestations are the unfolding of the results that we desire or have affirmed.

Affirmation (*Mindset*): Affirmation is a tool used to promote self-motivation and positive self-talk. This tool is what we use to build up the courage, and to put in the work needed to achieve our desired outcomes. These intentional statements and desires can help us to manifest what we want in the near and far future. Affirmations also focuses on our present mental state. Keep in mind that our mindset will always affect our present and future actions and experiences.

    It is true that affirmations are positive and encouraging statements. However, they are not one size fits all. If it doesn't feel authentic to who you desire to be, then that specific affirmation isn't for you. Affirmations symbolizes hopefulness, it does not fix lives. But with the right mindset, it will influence the way you deal with uncomfortable situations. Lastly, if it causes you to suppress, or invalidate your emotions, it is known as *toxic positivity*, not affirmations.

__Meraki Note:__ Affirmations are most effective when personalized, or when it truly resonates with you, your desires, and your current circumstances. Be sure to know that:

- *Generic mantras ≠ Intentional affirmations*
- *Toxic positivity ≠ Intentional affirmations*

Manifestation (*Reality*): To manifest something means to show a feeling by your actions or demonstrations. To me, this aligns with the bible scripture that says, "faith without works is dead." In this context it means that, affirmation without action is just meaningless positive words.

    Manifestation is what happens <u>because</u> of affirmation. It is the process that uses your thoughts and emotions to create your reality. When you are manifesting something, it requires you to <u>believe</u> that what you want is possible to achieve.

Meraki Note 1: Speaking things into existence/reality:

- *Speaking = Affirming*
- *Reality = Manifested*

Meraki Note 2: *Manifesting something will always require putting actions behind your affirmations.*

Positive words and mindset → Actions that aligns with mindset → Manifesting your desired reality

Meraki Journal Exercise: *Please find the Affirmation and Manifestation activity in your Meraki Journal. Affirmation creates a positive mindset. While manifestation uses that positive mindset to create your reality.*

Another bible scripture states that "death and life are in the power of the tongue". Meaning that, regardless of what you speak—whether negative or positive—it will be manifested into your life. I encourage you to affirm positive things, and positive things will happen to and around you. Don't allow your reality to be the results of procrastination, excuses, hate, insecurity, or unforgiveness. Let's be more intentional about what we say, and how we feel about ourselves and our lives.

Glorifying The Struggle

In addition to intentionally affirming things into our lives, we have to be careful of cultural quotes that has been passed down from generation to generations. Growing up, one of my favorite quotes was "what doesn't kill you, makes you stronger". But as I've gotten older and wiser, I've come to realize that this quote has influenced me to believe that struggling, or living pass a difficult time in my life equates to strength.

I want you to understand that you can survive something without gaining any strength or wisdom at all. Yes, it is possible to just make it out of a tough situation alive, and that is it. And sometimes, you can even come out of a situation weaker than you were before. Surviving struggles doesn't make you stronger. I believe that this generational statement became a mental abusive way of coercing myself, and others to associate struggle with strength. This type of <u>toxic positive mindset</u> is where the strong black women stigma keeps its power.

<u>Toxic Positivity</u>

Toxic positivity comes from feeling uncomfortable, and dismissive of unpleasant emotions. Demonstrating toxic positivity is when you force a positive mindset, or action to shut down appropriate reactions to a negative experience. For example, forcing yourself to be brave and strong in moments when, what you actually may need is comfort or a mental break. Being brave and strong is a beautiful thing, but it may not be beneficial in every moment. As the name suggest, toxic positivity is often <u>well-intentioned</u>, but can cause alienation, and a feeling of disconnection. Toxic positivity can also involves responding to distress with false reassurance rather than empathy. For example, telling yourself "I got this", when the appropriate response should be to ask for help.

<u>Meraki Note:</u> *Toxic positivity is voluntary dissociative behavior*

Ways of manifesting self-toxic positivity:

◊ Masking your true feelings
◊ Being in denial
◊ Experiencing the guilt of your true feelings
◊ Having the "just get on with it" mentality
◊ Being dismissive of your emotions
◊ Invalidating your authentic emotional experiences
◊ Minimizing your own feelings

<u>Meraki Note:</u> *Realize that it isn't the trauma that makes us stronger, kinder, and more compassionate. It's how we handled it. It's how we're healing from it. It's how we love ourselves through it. It's how we forgive, despite our pain. And it's how we treat others, on our good and bad days.*

<u>Strength Vs. Survival Mode</u>

Please note that survival mode isn't the same as strength

There are life-changing benefits that comes with knowing the differences between being strong and being in your survival mode. Your survival mode can cause you to become numb from feeling the pain of your trauma and hurt. When operating in your survival mode, you may seem strong from the outside looking in. And some days, you may even convince yourself that you are strong. Only because you have mistaken your numbness for strength.

Strength isn't granted when you get through a tough situation. Rather, an individual shows true strength when they're heal from what a tough situation attempted to destroy, or kill. Strength is when you succeed at regaining, or protecting what the enemy was trying to steal from you through your trauma. And most times, the target is your humanity, your heart, your smile, your joy, your confidence—*anything that will take power away from evil.*

<u>Meraki Note:</u> *Strength is demonstrated by applying the wisdom gained from the struggle.*

<u>Routine Vs. Consistency</u>

The trick is to set a routine, until you are able to be consistent.

     According to Pastor Stephanie Ike, routine and consistency can look the same, but the difference between the two is in your heart posture. Having a routine is to do something ritualistically because it may be required of us, in order to produce a specific outcome. Consistency is what we demonstrate when something becomes our lifestyle. For example, an individual who says an affirmation every day when they wake up in the morning, no matter what, most likely has a routine. And an individual who says affirmations a few times out of the week, or whenever they feel like they need a boost of self-confidence, is most likely exercising consistency. Please remember that in many cases, words and actions tend to lose their power when they are used ritualistically. So, be mindful that you don't let your affirmation become a routine. Rather, use your affirmation consistently.

<u>Meraki Note:</u> *Routine: I drink 3 bottles of water every day. 1 in the morning, 1 in the afternoon, and 1 two hours before bed. Consistency: I make sure that I am hydrated throughout the day.*

Part 2: Transitioning From A Liability Through Self-Love

Self-love requires self-acceptance:

⇒ Self-acceptance is having sympathy and compassion for yourself, but then doing what it takes to produce a better outcome. Without the second part, you are in jeopardy of displaying self-pity instead of self-acceptance.

Our Why: When you accept who you are, and what you have been through, you will interpret your experiences as learning opportunities, rather than something to be ashamed of. When you are ashamed of the things that you've been through, you're less likely to share those experiences with others. Which may cause you to miss opportunities to educate, encourage, and/or help those who may be experiencing what you have already lived through.

2.A The Art Of Self-Love

Loving yourself requires knowing your self-worth.

Meraki Note: *Most times, fear, anxiety, and self-doubt stems from not truly knowing your worth, and all that you are capable of. Which can lead to intense insecurities and low self-esteem.*

      I strongly believe that no amount of bad experiences can override self-love. When we love someone, we are more patient, more kind, more forgiving, and more gracious towards them. This concept is no different from true self-love. Yes, there may be a lot of negative events that has taken place in your life. To the point where you may believe that nothing good will ever happen to you; that you will never experience true happiness; and that you are unworthy of your heart's desires.

But love has the power to shift perspectives. If you believe that there is nothing about you that can cultivate self-love, you are wrong. Regardless of what you've been through, what you're currently experiencing, or how you envision your future unfolding, know that you are extremely worthy of genuine self-love. There's beauty, strength, love, charisma, intelligence, and so much more coursing through your veins. You are priceless. You are unique. And you are a gift to this world.

Here are some ways to assist you in cultivating self-love:

1. Become knowledgeable on what true self-love is.
    a. Read books about self-love
    b. Listen to interviews and podcasts about self-love

In hearing and reading about other people's journey to self-love, you are exposing your mind to the topic. When you feed your mind with a specific topic or content, you will slowly find yourself becoming open to the possibilities. This is the power of influence. Growing up as a Christian, we were always told to '*stay in the word*', which simply means to maintain the habit of reading the bible daily, or as much as possible. The elders of the church weren't instructing this because they thought we would forget what we've read. They believe that staying in the word will cultivate or influence a specific type of mindset.

2. Think of at least one person who you love dearly
    a. Write down all the reasons why you love them

        i. Their personality traits
       ii. Attributes
     iii. Physicality, etc.
  b. After completing this list, highlight everything that is similar, identical, or complementary to your traits and attributes

This is a simple, but important activity to do when you feel like you can't find anything about yourself to love. In doing so, you will quickly realize that the issue isn't that there isn't anything to love about yourself. The issue is that you're subconsciously bias against yourself, or for some reason, uncomfortable with being kind to yourself.

Meraki Note: *Some may believe that you shouldn't need a specific reason to love yourself. And overall, I agree with that statement. However, I also believe that we are all different, with our own experiences and struggles. We all have to start somewhere. So, if you have to think of specific reasons to love yourself at first, then by all means. I am proud of you for being unconventional, and creative in how you find self-love.*

Self-Worth

Self-worth isn't talked about enough. But if we take a moment to analyze the many issues that we face, we may realize that self-worth is the root of a lot of the issues. As humans there are many things that we may feel unworthy of. And there are many reasons that we may feel unworthy. Now, it may seem like I have written the same statement twice, but in different ways. However, that isn't the case. For example, we can feel unworthy <u>of love</u> *because* we may have been neglected as a child.

Meraki Note: *You can feel unworthy of many other things because of your childhood neglect. In the same way that you can have many other reasons why you feel unworthy of love. So, when dealing with the feeling of unworthiness, it's very important to figure out what you feel unworthy <u>of</u> and <u>why</u>.*

Below, we will discuss a few <u>reasons</u> for feeling unworthy. However, in your Meraki Journal, you will be prompted to discuss things that you feel unworthy <u>of</u>, and the reasons that has caused you to feel that way.

<u>Self-Worth And Past Experiences</u>

      Throughout the years we have been taught that our worth isn't based on how others may feel about us. Our worth is defined by how we feel about ourselves. But what happens when we are the ones who don't value our own selves? What if we truly believe that our worth is lower than what others see within us? What if we are the ones who believe that we are less than? Now, who's opinion is correct? Can we truly say that our worth is defined by how we feel about ourselves?
      Before answering these questions, first ask yourself, "why am I unworthy", better yet, ask yourself, "why am I worthy?" When you are answering these questions, I would like for you to change your <u>*I'm worthy because...*</u> to <u>*I'm worthy in spite of...*</u>

I need you to understand that you are worthy, no matter what.
      Many times when we struggle with low self-worth, it's usually because of our past experiences. I want to let you know that no matter what others may believe about you, or what you have experienced in the past, you are worthy. Even you can be wrong about your worth. Your

worth should not be influenced by any external factors. Therefore, if your opinion about yourself is influenced by what you have been through, then I would like to think that your opinion is incorrect. Your self-worth should be tied to your self-love, and your self-love should be unconditional.

There are life experiences and traumas that you had zero control over or desire for, which have deeply scarred you. Though those factors of your past have absolutely nothing to do with your self-worth, you may still be punishing yourself, because of your unjust association to your worth. Thus, giving yourself a life sentence in a prison of insecurities, anxiety, self-doubt, and low self-esteem. Please never forget that your worth isn't attached to anything that you go through in life, whether you had control over the situation or not.

Become aware of the many influencers of your <u>sense</u> of self-worth, you become more equipped to make the appropriate changes.

Some of these changes may be to:

- Eliminate or minimize access from factors that influences you to view yourself as less than
- Feed your mind with positive, kind, and encouraging words
- Surround yourself with people who nurture and highlight the best parts of you
- Surround yourself with people who aren't enablers

In moving forward, your worth should strictly be defined by how you love and protect yourself. How you show up for yourself. How you treat others, especially when you don't benefit from it. And what you accept and tolerate for yourself. Every chance you get, remind yourself that you are worthy of your heart's desires. You are worthy for bigger and better. You are worthy of peace and happiness. You are worthy of true freedom. You are worthy of all of the benefits that comes with being healed from all hurt and traumas. You are worthy of forgiveness. And you are worthy of unconditional love.

Self-Worth And Perceptions Of Others

A father bought his daughter a car as a present for graduating. He said, "Before I give it to you, take it to a car dealer in the city, and see how much they will offer you for it." When the girl spoke to the car dealers, they offered her $10,000 because the car looked very old." So, the father said, "Ok, take it to the pawn shop." When the girl arrived, the pawn shop owner offered her $1,000 because the car is very old, and needs a lot of work done." The father then told her to join a passionate car club with experts, and show them the car. Once the girl drove to the passionate car club, multiple club members offered her $100,000 because the car is rare, and in good condition." Then the father said, "I wanted to let you know that you are not worth anything, if you are not in the right place. If you are not appreciated, it just means that you are in the wrong place. Don't stay in a place where you are not valued."

Meraki Note: *This mini story is significant because it teaches us that our true worth is not based on the perceptive of others. The way we view or value each other is oftentimes based off of our own experience, knowledge, and point or view.*

We have to understand that when we put the faith of our self-worth into the hands of others, we are no longer in control of the only thing that God has given us complete control over—which is ourselves. Once you are truly in control of your narrative, and your sense of worth, your perception of others will evolve. You would soon realize that people's view of you is through the lens of their own level of maturity and beliefs. Once you realize this, it will be much easier for you to no longer waste your time, by trying to convince anyone of your worth and your truth.

People will judge, compare, and class you based on how they view themselves. For example, I am 5 feet and 3 inches tall. At this height, if I consider myself as tall, it is safe to say that anyone else who is taller than I am, I will also view as tall. Though I may argue that an individual who is 5'2 may be short. It is human nature to class others based on our own knowledge and perception of ourselves. So please understand that, whenever you start to feel your self-worth lessening after hours of scrolling on social media, it isn't because you all of a sudden became unworthy. It would be because you are comparing the distance of where you are in life, to where others may be saying, or showing that they are in their lives.

As mentioned before, be confident enough to know that others' successes should never take away from any progress that you have been making. Root for their success as much as you are rooting for yours. Know that their wins should not derail you from your own successes. It should only motivate, inspire, and encourage you to keep pushing forward.

And remember that the purity of how you celebrate other's successes should never be contingent on where you are in your own journey to success. Meaning, don't wait until you are succeeding, to celebrate others. Still celebrate others, even when things aren't necessarily going the best for you. We are all uniquely made by God, and we have our own purpose and attributes to offer to the world.

Meraki Note: *No matter what the level of your self-worth is, you should never put anyone down to make yourself feel or look better. **Trying** to put others down only proves that you truly believe in your heart, that they are better than you are—whether you want to admit it or not.*

Self-Worth And Cultural Trends

In fear of not fitting in or being looked down on, many may consciously or subconsciously invest in items that they may otherwise not have been interested in. They may align themselves with specific people to boost their images, or post heavily filtered pictures that resembles false perfection. Each time we do this, it eats away at our authenticity; causing us to slowly disassociate from our true worth. Because of this, we have contributed to a culture that deems it normal to compare each other, make stereotypical trends, and judge others based on the fixed unrealistic standards of what life should look like.

Sadly, more and more, our sense of worth has become so closely aligned with, or dependent on how the world sees us. While, completely disregarding our initial untainted truths about ourselves. This is unfortunate because the cultural standard of beauty relies on trends that are constantly changing. Therefore, if we associate our worth to culture, our self-love will not be founded on a solid foundation.

Meraki Note: *Many years ago, a cultural trend was to have very thin eyebrows. Now, the trend is to have full eyebrows. This is just a simple example to reiterate that, if you buy into the cultural standard of beauty, you will always find yourself playing tug of war with your self-worth and image.*

Self-Worth And Your Successes

Never align your self-worth to what culture defines as success. Success cannot be defined as a destination, or the possession of things. Real success isn't measured by how far you *are* in life. It's measured by how far you've *come,* in relations to where you have started. So, never discredit your success or progress, just because it doesn't look like what society says success is.

Scenario: Tracy was a homeless woman who somehow seized an opportunity to get herself straightened out. She received a job, where she is paid the minimum wage in her city. However, her monthly salary is enough to pay for her rent, cover her bills, and buy food each month. So, after showing proof of income, Tracy finally got approved for a small cozy apartment, not too far away from her job. Tracy went from being homeless, to having a comfortable place to rest, take nice warm showers, and have home cooked meals every day.

Ariel is a young woman who grew up in a home with two loving parents, where they provided a great life for her. She had the luxury of not having to work until she graduated college. Throughout her young adulthood, she has never gone a day hungry or without a warm shower. She has always been able to buy herself designer bags, shoes, and clothes whenever she pleased. And once she was ready to work, she was hired at her mother's successful company.

If you saw these two women's life on social media— without knowing their backstories, which one of them would you consider to be successful?

Scenario Continues...: Although Tracy started her day on a high note, feeling very proud of herself for how far she's come; it all changed once she stumbled upon Ariel's Instagram page. Before this moment, she has never met, or spoken to Ariel before. Tracy was so captivated by the lifestyle of Ariel, so much so, that she spent about an hour scrolling through her pictures and videos. As the minutes went by, she began to sink deeper and deeper into a quicksand type of depression. She couldn't help but to compare her life to the content that was displayed on Ariel's page. As the feeling of unworthiness slowly started to creep in, she said to herself, *"I can't wait 'til I'm as successful as her."*

This is disheartening because the truth of the matter is, based on the information given about the two women, Tracy has experienced success far more times than Ariel did. Once again, true success is an accomplishment of something. A progression from one point to another.

Meraki Note: *This scenario isn't about putting anyone down, or insulting the easy life. This scenario is only meant to highlight what the true meaning of success is.*

For far too long, we have gotten it all wrong. Being able to buy designer things isn't the meaning of success. Stop allowing others to pressure you into believing that you have to be a certain way, or have certain things, in order to see yourself as successful. Aspire to be like someone who is actually elevating and progressing. Aspire to emulate someone who is striving for generational health and wealth. Aspire to follow the footsteps of people who pride themselves on investing in assets, and minimal liabilities. Aspire to be like someone who lives for happiness, and not for objects.

Meraki Exercise: *Ask yourself:*

- *Does my image or self-worth rely on what I'm exposed to daily?*
- *Am I enforcing healthy boundaries?*
- *Would I feel this way about myself if there weren't any media, or trend opposing this specific thing about me?*
- *Is my self-worth dependent on people and/or circumstances?*
- *Would this opinion of myself change if it suddenly becomes the most popular thing in the culture?*

Meraki Note: *Remember to be completely honest with yourself when asking these questions. And no matter what your answers are, don't be too harsh on yourself. Meet yourself where you're at, and move on from there. Take a moment to brainstorm ways of how to safely transition out of this unhealthy mindset.*

Whether it's to:

- *Set better boundaries*
- *Self-reflect*
- *Affirm yourself*
- *Surround yourself with nurturing people*

2.B Self-Love: C.H.A.R.T.S

Taking pride in who you are, and where you are mentally and physically is a big part of self-love.

In the Meraki Journey, there are six main attributes of self-love, which is the **C.H.A.R.T.S** that we will follow in cultivating, and maintaining the healthiest forms of self-love. The six attributes of self-love are **C**aring, **H**onesty, **A**ctivating The **P.U.S.H.** Mentality, **R**esilience, **T**reasuring, and **S**ecurity of Mind.

Meraki Note: *Self-love isn't about accepting everything about yourself, as if there isn't anything to be changed. Self-love is recognizing what needs to be changed, and loving yourself enough to do something about it.*

<u>Self-Love = Care</u>

Unwind, relax your mind, and love on yourself.

     Not allowing anyone to disturb your peace, is a part of self-care. Self-care is the act of catering to your body, mind, and spirit. Many of us have heard the saying that self-care is sanity, not vanity. I love this saying because it wittily encourages us, to never allow anyone to guilt trip us out of doing what we believe is best for ourselves. Oftentimes, when we finally decide to choose ourselves in a situation, we are met with words like selfish and vain. In these moments, it is wise to reinforce your boundaries, and remind yourself that people's perceptions are based on their level of understanding.

Meraki Note: *There are two types of self-care, which are self-care days and self-care breaks.*

     Self-care breaks are more closely related to prioritizing yourself. While self-care days are more closely related to spoiling, or treating yourself. <u>Self-awareness</u> will allow you to discern which type of self-care is needed in each moment. Though both are very important, Meraki Journey will be focusing more on self-care breaks; because I believe that self-care breaks are necessary in your healing and self-transformational journey. While self-care days are necessary in maintaining the positive results that you've gain throughout the journey.

Self-care days are about putting nonessential responsibilities on pause, and doing what centers, calms, and rejuvenates you. On these days, if it doesn't bring you happiness, love, peace, or positive energy, this is not the day for it. Self-care days are usually planned—weekly, biweekly, or monthly. These type of days, not only gives you the chance to be away from people and things that drains your positive energy. It also gives you the chance to pour back into yourself. By restocking your energy, patience, peace, love, and anything else that you've been drained of during the week(s).

Self-care days oftentimes include:

- Spa activities
- Lunch or dinner dates
- Trips
- Full days of doing anything that adds to your happiness

On the other hand, self-care breaks can be a daily exercise that may range anywhere between minutes, days, or weeks. The time frame of your breaks should depend on your sought-after affects, and what you are taking a break from. Self-care breaks are usually not planned. However, if you are the type to always be on the go, and sometimes forget to check in with self, making it a routine to take self-care breaks is essential. Make it a routine, until it becomes your lifestyle.

Self-care breaks can include:

- Long walks
- Listening to motivational or inspirational podcasts
- Journaling
- Reading educational books
- Setting and working towards your short-term and long-term goals
- Finding new hobbies
- Exercising
- Learning something new—such as a new language, sport, or skill.

Meraki Note: *Your breaks, and alone time should also include exposing yourself to different sceneries and cultures, that stimulate your mind to be inspired, productive, imaginative, and to dream big.*

These breaks are perfect opportunities to become more in-tuned with yourself. And to learn more about who you are, in ways that you may not be able to, during the moments when you are too available to outside noises and distractions. As mentioned before, self-care breaks are also about taking the time to check in with yourself, ensuring that your cup is still full, and your peace is still abundant.

Self-Love = Honesty

One of the main attributes of self-love is honesty. We can all agree that dishonesty is one of the first links to a broken bond, or a tainted connection in any type of relationship. So, I encourage you to honor the bond that you are creating with yourself, by being truthful with yourself through self-love and self-respect.
Some truths that you can start with are:

- I am not where I want to be yet, but I will put in the effort needed to get there.
- I am not okay, but I know better days are coming.
- Today, my faith feels smaller than a mustard seed, what can I do to make it better?
- I'm disappointed in my body image, so today I will create a healthy plan and stay consistent this time.

Meraki Note 1: *The key to self-honesty is to always state a solution, encouraging statement, or a positive follow-up question that may lead to a solution, or trigger the growth of your critical thinking skills. When you use this technique, it kills the spirit of self-pity, and the habit of useless complaining.*

Meraki Note 2: *Stating a problem without a follow-up question, solution, or encouragement, is simply just stating a complaint.*

However, being honest with yourself doesn't always have to involve a problem. There are many truths about you and your life that is 100% positive. Some of those truths can be:

- I am fearfully and wonderfully made.
- I'm doing awesome today.
- I love my eyes, my smile, and my personality.
- I am worthy of all the love that I receive throughout my lifetime.

Meraki Note: *Positive truths can include compliments, encouragements, and affirmations.*

Oftentimes, we are dishonest with ourselves, to avoid the quilt that may come with being fully honest. For example, you may dread the guilt that comes with admitting that you need a mental break from your kids, and/or partner. You may feel guilty for admitting it because of how much you love them. But I want you to find solace in knowing that you are doing yourself and your loved ones a favor, when you are honest about needing a mental break.

Keep in mind that it is impossible to be the best parent and lover, if you aren't the best version of yourself. So, please take the time needed to check-in on yourself and regroup. In admitting that you aren't okay, you are either giving yourself a reason to seek help, make some healthy changes, or give your loved ones the opportunity to give you the support that you need.

Girl Boss to Boss Mom
By: London Heflin

As I sit here and write this letter to you beautiful queens, my newborn baby girl is asleep in my arms, and my 3-year-old son is playing with his cars and screaming siren sounds. In a perfect world, I would be writing this in peace and quiet, but you know how that goes! I share this with you because as a boss mom, there is no perfect world! We make things work with what we have, and we make it look effortless! I know you're tired girl. I know you're mentally and physically drained. I know that deep down in your heart, you want to ask for help, but you just feel like you can do it all! I know you have work to do, and your tasks are piling up by the day; because simply put, you have no time for it! Whether you work a 9-5 or you're an entrepreneur like me, it gets tough trying to balance work and motherhood! It's like having two full time jobs and quite frankly, you can't quit either one!

I'm here to tell you that even though it is tough, it gets better & YOU get better! You learn different techniques that work for you, to take care of your kiddies & also get your work done. You get your own groove and

rhythm, and you learn to shut out unwanted opinions. You do things YOUR way because you are a Boss Mom! Things are different from when you were a girl boss & that's okay! That girl boss was shaking things up, and making ways for the Boss Mom in you to move mountains! You are raising a child or children, and that my love, is NOT for the faint! So give yourself grace, love on yourself, treat yourself, and remind yourself daily that you are enough, and you are doing your absolute best!
Self-love is the best love and always remember, your kid(s) don't need a perfect mom, they need a happy one!

Stay bossed up queens!

-London Heflin

Self-Love = Activating The P.U.S.H. Mentality

***P.U.S.H.** past **p**sychological traps with **p**atience, **u**nderstanding, **s**toutheartedness, **h**opefulness*

If not all, many of us, have felt the feeling of the walls closing in on us. This feeling can be triggered or influenced by various types of experiences. Causing us to feel cluster phobic and trapped within ourselves. At times, you may feel stuck or frustrated, because of the overwhelming effects of financial strains, health deficiencies, relationship issues, or other things that might be too difficult to speak about. Feeling like the walls are closing in on you, can also happen when you experience prolong discomfortable in your own sacred spaces.
So, what do you do to relieve yourself from feeling like the walls are closing in on you? How do you cope when there isn't any peace in your home? What do you do when no matter where you go, you can't seem to escape the suffocating feeling of those walls closing in?

*The same thing that you would naturally do if a physical wall was closing in on you. You **P.U.S.H**. back.*

When we aren't experiencing comfort, freedom, peace, or happiness in our own mental or physical sacred spaces, we tend to seek immediate escapes. Which, in most cases, are very temporary or counterproductive. So, instead of being so quick to escape from yourself by any means necessary, tap into the very essence of what makes you resilient, and P.U.S.H. pass your mental traps. In moments like these, self-love is about be patient with yourself. Being understanding of your assignment. Being stouthearted— courageous, determine, and bold. And being hopeful.

Patience:

Sometimes, we may feel trapped within ourselves because we are in such a rush to get out of a situation. Not realizing that the purpose of the situation, may be to teach us valuable and necessary lessons for our future endeavors. Yes, this season of your life may be extremely uncomfortable for you, but I want to encourage you to practice patience. Take this time to focus on learning all the lessons that this season is meant to offer you. And—you never know—maybe, this is the only way to truly escape from what you're dealing with.

Sometimes, being strong and fighting for yourself may not look like what we are used to fighters looking like. On days when you are feeling overwhelmed and drained from all that you've been going through, the best thing to do is to take a moment to acknowledge what you are feeling, and be patient with yourself. Remember that it's never okay to stifle or dismiss how you genuinely feel. Once you have acknowledged and dealt with your emotions, it will now become harder for the enemy to use your feelings against you.

Remember that the lesson you struggle with will repeat itself until you learn from it, and make the appropriate changes. So, instead of using your energy to throw a fit, isolate yourself, lash out on others, or repeatedly victimize yourself; slow down, take things one step at a time, and learn what needs to be learned in order to elevate to the next level of your life.

Understanding:

When you are feeling trapped within yourself, and not sure what your next move should be, try to understand who you are. I know that this may be an odd thing to say for a situation like this. However, sometimes when you don't know what to do in specific situations, it can be because you aren't aware of the tools that are available to you.

Self-Reflection Questions:

- What have I learned in a previous phase of my life that can help me out of this situation?
- Is there an overlooked skillset that I've gain in the past, that can help me right now?
- Have I been through something similar to this before?
- If so, how did I deal with it?
- Who do I have in my corner that can be a resource for solving my issue?

Also, take a moment to understand where you are in life, and where you want to be in the near and far future. Assess, and plan the journey that will get you from where you currently are, to where you want to be. And the moment your waiting season is over, you will already be well equipped to make your first move. Instead of wasting your first moments of *freedom*, by trying to get yourself ready to make the first move.

Game Plan:

1) Understand the situation that you are dealing with
2) Assess and analyze what has triggered the walls to close in
    a. This will give you the confidence to calmly think of healthy solutions.
3) Acknowledge your feelings
4) Remind yourself of your own bravery by giving yourself credit for making it this far.
    a. You are a conqueror, an achiever, and a fighter. You didn't come this far to only come this far. Though very cliché, is it true? Yes.
5) Draft potential solutions in your Meraki Journal.

Stoutheartedness:

Though the self-transformational process prompts you to be in control of yourself, and what you allow in your life. It takes solid bravery to stay in control of yourself when your circumstance is out of your control. And you feel like your life is suffocating you. Be courageous enough to say to yourself, "while I do what I can to better myself for the next stage of my life, I will honor the purpose of this waiting season".

Each time that you say this to yourself, try to believe it a little more than you did the previous time. And in due time, you will get to a point where your words will no longer be needed as a reminder. Because your actions will have already started to demonstrate this statement over and over again.

Affirmation ➔ Manifestation

Hopefulness:

It is a given that no one likes to feel restricted, trapped, or stuck. However, your waiting or wilderness seasons are meant to teach you valuable lessons for the next stage of life. Knowing that this period is supposed to teach you valuable lessons, should give you hope. Lessons means that *there is life after this*. It should give you the hope that something bigger, and more incredible is coming to you. And it should also give you hope that God is gifting you this season as a little extra time, to pack on more knowledge, more self-love, more wisdom, and more discernment. So that you will be well equipped to be a testament to others. When we are hopeful for what's to come, it motivates us to stay in the fight. To not give up on ourselves. And to prepare ourselves for what's next.

Self-Love = Resilience

Yes, there will be days where you'll feel overwhelmed, drained, misunderstood, taken for granted, or unappreciated. There will be days where you'll feel plagued with so many triggering emotions all at once. There will be days where you'll find it very difficult to determine why you are experiencing these negative feelings. There will be days when you can't seem to locate the area of your life that is causing these emotions. And there will also be days when finding effective solutions, to rectify these feelings, will feel impossible. Causing you to fall into depression, and many other dark states of mind.

On days like these, I encourage you to dig deep, and find even the tiniest reason to hold on. On days like these, don't worry about how God will use you to help others, or even how you will get out of whatever situation you may be in. I encourage you to focus the tiniest bit of energy that you have left, to fight for your sanity and survival. And if you ever feel that you don't have anything to fight for, know that your younger self is rooting for you, and your older self can't wait to finally meet you.

So, though many may have been disappointed you in the past, do your best to not disappoint yourself—any version of yourself. And one day you're going to look back on how you held on, despite feeling like you didn't have anything left within you. You're going to feel so proud and elated that you didn't give up.

Through it all, never forget that you are, and have always been an element that defines uniqueness, resilience, stoutheartedness, and courage. Though sometimes you may not feel like it, always remember that you are truly loved. It doesn't matter if it's one, five, twenty, five hundred, or a million people who love you. Hold on to the few who truly love you—including yourself, and never let go.

<u>Self-Love = Treasure</u>

There are many ways to treasure yourself. However, one of the most important ways to do so is to ask for help when needed. This attribute of self-love is rarely spoken about, because it goes against so many trends of our culture, such as the "I can do bad all by myself", "Ms. Independent", "I'm a man, I got this", and even the "strong black women" brand. Through personal experiences, and the experiences of others, we have learned the harsh lesson of being our own superheroes. But I want to encourage you to treasure yourself enough to not self-sabotage your growth, or success because of the stigmas behind asking for help.

Once you have done the work to surround yourself with trustworthy, genuine, and loving people, try to get use to letting your guard down a bit, and ask for the help that you need. I understand that you may feel reluctant to ask for help when needed because of past disappointments, mistrust, betrayals, or letdowns. You may feel fearful of being a burden to others. Or perhaps the hesitation in asking for help, is because of the expectations that have already been set for you by others. Causing you to feel a sense of guilt, or failure if you do ask for help.

I want to let you know that asking for help doesn't mean that you have failed at anything. Failure is when your mind has the ability to be honest with you; but instead of listening to it, you ignore its plea to you to ask for help. Please, don't fail yourself. Trust that your mind and body knows how much you can take, before rendering unhealthy.

Though I salute you for trying to handle certain things all on your own, I need you to know that there is a difference between taking care of your problems like a boss, and drowning in your problems because of your fears. Don't sit there trapped in your own thoughts. Trying to convince yourself that it's best to rely on your own strengths. Know that you matter, and seek the help that you know you truly need and deserve.

<u>Self-Love = Security Of Mind</u>

Our mind is the most powerful element of self. So, let's secure it.

For a moment, let's think of your mental security as a physical being. Your mental security is activated the moment you were born. It is in charge of keeping your mind from being easily frustrated, having clouded thoughts, or making tainted decisions. When you feed your mind with thoughts of being unworthy, focusing on negative experiences, harboring unchecked emotions, unforgiveness, and jealousy, you are decaying and disabling your mental security. *Each negative thought is like a virus that breaks*

down your mind's security bit by bit.
Be intentional about supporting the security, that is tasked with keeping your mind guarded and safe.

The best way to do this is to engage in:

- Positive self-talk
- Documenting your thoughts and emotions
- Authentic words of affirmation
- Choosing you company wisely
- Creating a physical or mental sacred space where you can find peace

How can a clean environment improve your mind's security?

Being organized will allow you to effortlessly spot anything that needs to be rooted out. When your home or mind is cluttered, it represents things that have been swept under the rug, a lack of discipline, chaos, confusion, and other unchecked liabilities. Being organized promotes clear thinking, refreshes your mood, and allows a shift in your perspective.

The state of your mental security is what sets the tone for your day. A clean and organized mind and space will decrease the chances of you becoming overwhelmed. Have you ever noticed how frustrated you get with unrelated situations, when there is chaos or cluster in your mind or home? Have you ever felt an immediate renewal of the mind, after taking a moment to clean up, or organize your space or thoughts? Cleanliness and organization are the keys to strong and healthy mental security.

Conceit Vs. Self-Love:

In order for us to give ourselves the purest version of self-love, we must first learn the many differences between being conceded and exuding self-love. Unlike the examples of self-love, conceit rarely involves any negative truths, solutions, or positive critical thinking. Conceitedness is an unjustified feeling of being pleased with yourself. It's your responsibility to always be humble. However, never allow the fear of being accuse of conceitedness cause you to dim your light. Be proud of all the hard work that you have done on yourself. And be proud of who you are as a whole.

Please do not wait on others to encourage, motivate, or compliment you in order for you to feel good about yourself, or to have a good day.

Part 3: Becoming An Asset Through Self-Care

3.A Prioritizing Vs. Spoiling

As I have mentioned before, there are two types of self-care. Which are self-care <u>breaks</u> and self-care <u>days</u>.

- Self-care breaks = Prioritizing self = Keeping your cup full
- Self-care days = Spoiling self = Maintaining an overflowing cup

<u>**Meraki Note:**</u> *Your cup is another word for yourself.*

Self-care breaks are more closely related to prioritizing yourself, while self-care days are more closely related to spoiling yourself. Although both are extremely important for the betterment of you, they should not be used interchangeably. There are distinct differences between prioritizing, and spoiling oneself. Spoiling yourself is what you do when you feel the need to <u>reward</u> yourself—by doing things outside of what you would do on a normal day.

On the other hand, prioritizing yourself is a consistent, daily form of self-care. It is the conscious decision to take a moment, to briefly recenter yourself, relax your mind, and keep your emotions in check, despite how busy or demanding your schedule may be.

Our Why:

When we mistake prioritizing ourselves for spoiling ourselves, we will mishandle our *cup*. We will engage in activities in hopes of refilling our cup, only when we are running low. As opposed to when we are no longer overflowing. As mentioned before, prioritizing yourself should keep your cup full. While spoiling yourself—*with an already full cup*—will help maintain your cup running over. This means that spoiling yourself shouldn't be the tool that is utilized in getting your cup full. It should be used to get your cup to an overflowing point, <u>*after*</u> it has already been filled, through the acts of prioritizing yourself each day.

Monitoring Your Cup: <u>Is Your Cup Full Or Empty?</u>

Know that everything you do will require you to give. In monitoring your cup, it is essential to know that giving is not limited to materialistic things or money. Giving can also be in the form of emotional or spiritual elements. Always keep in mind that whenever you interact with a partner, friends, kids, or family members, you are giving a part of yourself.

- You are pouring your wisdom into them, supporting them, and uplifting them.
- You are investing your time by staying on the phone with them
- You are spending quality time with them in person
- You are investing your energy by being a listening ear, and giving sound advice

Prioritizing yourself is a way for you to acknowledge that you also matter, and that your emotions, and feelings are valid. However, this doesn't mean that you forget about your loved ones, or your responsibilities. It simply means that you are protecting your mental, physical, emotional, and spiritual health, by making sure that you are only pouring from an overflowing cup versus, an empty cup.

Meraki Exercise: Take a moment to think about everyone you pour into, make sacrifices for, and always go the extra mile for.
    a. Write down all the names that have come to mind in numerical form
    b. Analyze the list from top to bottom.
    c. Circle or highlight your name.
    d. Which number did you list your name by?
    e. Is your name even on that list at all?
    f. Place your name at the top of that list.

In the words of Iyanla Vanzant, it's not selfish to put yourself first. Putting yourself first is known as being self-full. Hence, the reason for monitoring your cup is to make sure that you are only giving from your excess or overflow.

Be mindful that:

- If your name is closer to the bottom of your list, it implies that you may have been giving from an empty, or half-filled cup
- If your name isn't on the list at all, it implies that you tend to neglect yourself, in the name of helping others.
- If your name is the only name on the list, it implies that you mainly operate through selfishness
- If your name is at the top of the list, with multiple names following after, it implies that you are self-full. And giving from your excess.

This exercise may seem somewhat meaningless, but it is a visual representation that symbolizes a new commitment, and vow to making yourself a priority. You are making a vow to no longer overextend yourself, to the point where you are giving from what you actually need for your own survival.

How to fill your cup?

No one should ever feel comfortable with accepting from your survival kit. However, it is your responsibility to monitor your own cup.

Monitoring your cup involves:

- ♥ Setting and maintaining healthy boundaries
- ♥ Choosing your company wisely
- ♥ Exercising self-love daily
- ♥ Knowing your worth
- ♥ Taking self-care breaks daily

What's given to others?

What's running over should be what you freely give to others, whether it's your time, energy, money, or other resources. Remember that it is a beautiful thing to help others. However, you have to first get yourself to safety before you can help anyone else.

Meraki Note: *Don't run out into the war zone to retrieve anyone, knowing that what's in your oxygen tank isn't enough to get you back to where you'd be able to refill it.*

3.B Choose Your Company Wisely

Ships don't sink because of the water around them. They sink because of the water that gets inside of them. So, use your surroundings to get you to where you need to go. But it's who and what you allow in circle that will make or break your journey. Choosing your company wisely isn't an uncommon saying, by any means. But when it really comes down to it, do we actually take the time to choose our company wisely? Or do we go off of emotions, familiarity, and who is convenient for where we are in our lives currently?

Meraki Note: *Our company includes friends, family, lovers, and even coworkers who we interact with outside of a professional setting.*

Though we have complete control over our thoughts, perceptions, feelings, actions, and words, we are not immune to influence. Therefore, in order to create and maintain a positive mindset, we have to choose our company wisely. When actively choosing who we want to share our lives with, we should strive to be around people who we are equally yoked with us, or who inspires us to become better versions of ourselves.

All authentic relationships, whether platonic, romantic, or familial, consists of both parties influencing each other in positive ways—you influence them, as they influence you. This is why it is not only important for you to be ambitious, kind, innovative, and mature, it is equally important to be around individuals who share those qualities as well.

<u>Meraki Note:</u> *When you surround yourself with like-minded, and success-driven people, they won't see your achievements and milestones as bragging, as competition, or as the absence of their own successes. They will feel proud of you, they will celebrate you, and they may even become inspired to start, or to continue their own growth and achievements.*

Please note that if you are still struggling with low self-esteem, low self-love, self-doubt, and the inability to set healthy boundaries, choosing your company wisely will be close to impossible. If you want to have and keep good quality people in your life, you have to start by becoming a good quality person yourself. So I advise that you first focus on your own self-transformation and healing before <u>actively</u> trying to add people into your life.

Yes, you may already have good quality people in your life before you embark on your self-transformation and healing journey. And yes, people may enter your life during your journey. And that's amazing. However, please don't go <u>actively</u> seeking to add people into your life, while you are still struggling with your identity and traumas. Because you may put a potentially beautiful relationship in jeopardy of being nurtured by toxic habits, and a negative mindset.

Another reason to wait until you have healed, and

gain emotional and mental maturity is because you attract what you give out. If you actively try to seek company while in a low or dark space of your life, you are likely to attract friends and lovers who will bring more demons and trials that you will eventually need to overcome. Which ultimately delays your process of healing and self-transformation. Yes, I know that healing and elevating can feel very lonely, but know that this time of your life is not a permanent chapter. So, take advantage of this season by pouring into yourself, learning who you truly are, and mature as much as you can.

Meraki Note: *Your ultimate happiness could be delayed because of your desperate attempts to avoid feeling lonely, or the lack of implementing healthy boundaries.*

When choosing your company Wisely, pay close attention to:

- Their morals
- Their level and style of communication
- How they treat people who they can't benefit from
- How they carry themselves
- How they speak about themselves and others

When choosing your company Unwisely, you may choose people who:

- You think are great candidates to love you
- You believe can benefit your life in some way
- Provides some familiarity of your past—known as trauma bonding.
- Represent the negative thoughts, and views of yourself
- Match the image that you may be trying to advertise

Healthy relationships, and genuine human connections are extremely vital to the wellness of your mental and physical health. There is a parable that says, *don't be so thirsty for company, that you go around drinking from every cup. You may get yourself poisoned.* To me, this simply means that when you mindlessly go around connecting with just anyone, you are putting yourself in danger of exposing yourself to toxic influences. Whether it's the exposure to ideologies that may affect your spirit negatively; toxic words that has the power to kill your self-esteem; or negative energy that sucks the life out of your sacred spaces.

Taking your time to choose your company wisely, and being happy with having quality over quantity is so worth it. It makes a big difference when you have amazing people, with good intentions in your life. People who love you, care about you, and support your dreams. Kindhearted individuals who motivate, inspires, and celebrate you. People who share similar or aligned morals and values. And people who will exercise healthy communication skills with you. These are the individuals who deserve your love, your attention, and the support of their dreams.

Choose Your Company Through Logic

When choosing someone to be in your life, try your best to stay away from relying on potential. Do not romanticize the idea of what a person can be in your life, or what they can possibly bring to the table. When you do this, you are setting yourself up to be in a relationship with someone who may be completely different from the person you envisioned them to be. Also, never be so caught up in what you think an outcome will be like, to the point where you get distracted from exercising your discernment.

In other words, don't be so in love, infatuated, or

hopeful about someone, that you miss all the red flags. As said by Pastor Michael Todd, don't starve your discernment by feeding your distraction. Too often, we tend to sacrifice or ignore our discernment, all in the name of excitement, desires, goals, and potentials. When we are distracted by the potential effects of a *blessing*, we will miss the obvious red flags and deceptions.

Don't be so caught up with the potential of a friendship that you miss:

- The side eyes
- The jealousy
- The constant dark sarcasm
- Subtle jabs disguised as jokes
- The plotting against you

Don't be so caught up with the potential of a romantic connection that you miss the signs of:

- Domestic violence
- Actions and words not matching up
- Infidelity and deception

Maintaining Good Relationships

So far, when relationships have been mentioned, I've offered tools to deal with negative individuals. And advisements to first become a better version of yourself, in order to interact better with others. However, in the spirit of trying to cover as much ground as possible, it is essential note that every relationship will have its ups and downs. Still, it will require commitment, willingness, and effort for each relationship to work.

As you go through your self-transformational process, some individuals in your life may be on their own transformational journey as well. So the key to establishing a healthy relationship involves both parties discussing and agreeing on ways to continuously adapt, and support positive changes in each other. Encourage and celebrate each other's accomplishments, transformation, and wisdom gained.

3.C Is Communication Key?

I'm sure that we all have heard the saying, communication is key. But what is communication really the key of? Without comprehension, communication can quickly become the key to confusion and frustration.

    Let's picture two individuals communicating. One is speaking Japanese, while the other is speaking Spanish. The Japanese speaker and the Spanish speaker both have confirmed that they are indeed speaking to each other. But they also admitted that they can only understand a few words of the other language. These two individuals may be experiencing a high level of confusion. Similar to the confusion that two individuals who speak the same language, but still cannot understand each other's points of view would be experiencing.

    If we don't understand each other, what is the conversation really accomplishing? Successful communication isn't just about having the ability to hold a mature conversation. That's only half of it. The key to communicating well, is to also have the ability to comprehend what is being said to you. Which is why communication consists of two parts—speaking and listening.

Speaking:

With respect, speak <u>for the other person to understand</u> the point that you are trying to make, and the emotions that you are trying to convey. Try to never speak above anyone; even if you believe that that person isn't as educated, or as wise as you are. It's never okay to patronize, or to have a belittling session with anyone. On the other hand, though you shouldn't speak in ways that suggests that you are better, or more intelligent than the next person, never lower your communication skills in order to match the ignorance, shallowness, or disrespect that the other person may be spewing out. *Let's only try to match positive energy.*

Listening:

Communication isn't just about how you talk; it's about how you listen. Active listening shows that you not only heard what is being said, but that you are taking in and <u>processing</u> what they are saying. When respectfully listening, it's not okay to make facial or bodily expressions, that intimidates, discourages, or suggests invalidity to what they are saying. Calmly listen to respond to what is being said. Your response shouldn't be to deflect, or to say anything that doesn't address their words or concerns. Remember that your purpose for listening is to understand what they are saying, how they are feeling, and the points that they are trying to make. Give them the same courtesy and grace that you expect when you are the speaker.

Meraki Note: *When communicating to arrive at some sort of solution, the intent shouldn't be to suit one person. The solution should be suitable for the betterment of the <u>situation</u>. When this is the case, you will have a better chance of reaching a neutral solution, as opposed to a* *solution where one person's concerns are disregarded.*

Filtered Communication

Self-awareness and healing are the two first topics covered in the Meraki Journey. Because if you aren't healed from your past hurts and traumas, and you are unaware of your own behaviors and thought process, you are bond to communicate through the filter of your pain and ignorance. Yes, comprehension can be the key to a level-headed conversation. However, both parties have to be willing to arrive at solutions that are suitable for the situation at hand. As opposed to communicating with bitterness of unrelated, but similar past experiences.

On several occasions, I have mentioned that your feelings are always valid. That you should trust your own judgment, and stick to your word. And in the overall scope of things, I still agree with those statements to a certain extent. But if you are an individual who is still struggling with past hurts and traumas, this statement may be a little tricky. So, allow me to clarify. Sometimes, our feelings may be influenced by past traumas, hurts, and other experiences. When we have not healed, nor strengthened our minds to be truthful—without the filter of our past hurts—it will be extremely difficult to produce accurate feelings.

For example, a friend may have missed your call, and failed to return your call within a reasonable time frame, due to their own personal reasons. However, your feelings towards this action may be influenced by what you've been through in the past. Maybe in this moment you are still struggling with abandonment issues, due to your past experiences of neglect and abandonment. Or maybe this action has triggered a memory of a time when a delayed return call was directly linked to infidelity. So yes, you may have valid reasons for your feelings. However, your response to the <u>current</u> situation shouldn't be an attempt to address past experiences.

    This task may be very difficult to achieve for a while. And that's okay, as long as you are honestly trying to get better. However, in the meantime, I advise that you willingly offer meaningfully apologies, whenever you fail to separate your past and current experiences. I also advise that you surround yourself with people who are graceful and understanding of your struggles. Because this is where great communication skills on both sides will disarm your triggers.

    No, I don't believe that the people around you should accept this type of behavior from you forever. You have to make progress, and eventually get fully better. If you find yourself lashing out in ways that you most likely wouldn't have, if you were healed from similar past experiences, you need to take some time, to heal. This way, you can communicate maturely. And also, be free from past experiences that negatively control your feelings and reactions.

Gut Feelings

Sometimes, our gut feelings can be filtered through our past experiences as well.

    Sometimes our thought process and our gut feelings intertwine. The level of intuition or gut feelings that we have is based on how we feed, train, and nurture it. Though our gut in this context refers to a figurative gut, it shares similar characteristics of our physical body. No matter what we do, if we do it on a daily or consistent basis, our mind and body will eventually get used to it. Which causes us to sometimes operate without even putting much thought into it—like driving a car, or typing on a keyboard. This is known as muscle memory or *second nature*.

Because of our second nature tendencies, our mind may produce a specific gut feeling, in an attempt to keep us from experiencing similar outcomes, when dealing with familiar experiences. In many cases, this gut feeling can be inaccurate and misleading. So, when making decisions or dealing with familiar circumstances, make sure that what you are feeling is accurate and logical. Practice seeing things as they are. Not as how they use to be, or what they can be.

Meraki Note: *Regardless of the stage of your healing, your feelings should always be taken into consideration. However, it is good practice to make sure that your actions and reactions are reasonable, and warranted by the* <u>*current*</u> *situation.*

3.D Maintaining Healthy Relationships

In essence, relationships are supposed to be fulfilling, exciting, and meaningful. Yes, there will be ups and downs, and some may not grow at the same pace as their counterparts. However, if the difference in growth pace doesn't lead to negative emotions and behaviors in the relationship, I believe that it is worth keeping and nourishing.

Healthy Relationship Practices:

⇒ Become comfortable with conversing maturely
⇒ Don't be too quick to feel attacked, or taking things too personally
⇒ Don't be too quick to fall into defense mode
⇒ Have the courage to remain calm, and assertive
⇒ Don't always think that your way of doing things is always the right or best way

⇒ Be open to corrections, and willing to make appropriate changes

Meraki Note: *No one is perfect, and pretending to be, is very distasteful.*

Surrounding yourself with like-minded people doesn't mean that everyone around you will share the same goals and aspirations as you. Being connected with like-minded people indicates that you're both committed to working on self-development, self-love, and self-care. You're both committed to following your own goals and aspirations to better yourselves. You're both committed to putting equal effort into the relationship. And you're both committed to the **C.L.E.V.E.R** hack of maintaining a healthy relationship.

Meraki Journey's **C.L.E.V.E.R.** relationship hack:

- ∇ **Communicate with honesty and openness**
- ∇ **Love with authentic actions and intentions**
- ∇ **Encourage and celebrate growth and accomplishments**
- ∇ **Value each other's feelings**, *even when you believe that you're right*
- ∇ **Establish healthy boundaries**
- ∇ **Respectful healthy disagreements and point of views.**

Remember that each relationship in your life is unique. But what's constant should be a clear understanding of where you both stand with each other, and where the relationship is leading to. Also remember that, although a common goal in any relationship should be growth, your path to achieving your own personal growth may not be identical to their path to growth. So, never compare your journeys in a negative light. If anything, try to learn from each other's mistakes and accomplishments.

Part 4: Maintaining Through Self-Check-Ins

4.A Self-Control

At times, you may get overwhelmed and frustrated by things that aren't going your way. And at times, there may be situations that have gone so wrong around you, that you can't seem to get a grip on life long enough to control the situation. I need you to take a moment, and to come to terms with the lesson that you aren't in control of anything but yourself.

You are responsible for your words, your thoughts, your actions, your perceptions, and your feelings. Anything beyond those is out of your control. Yes, you have the power to manifest your dreams into reality; however, once it is out of you, it is out of your control. That is why it is so important to have a positive mindset, speak kind words, and improve your perception of your experiences. In doing so, you are able to lace your words and actions with as much power as you can before it is released from you.

Yes, it is your dreams; yes, it is your ideas; and yes, it is your plans. But once these elements are no longer within you, you can only partially be in control in certain situations. Simply because your actions and words can still influence outside elements positively, negatively, or even delay a process.

Meraki Note 1: *Please know that there's a difference between influencing something and controlling something.*

Meraki Note 2: *You can't control what others do to you. But you have 100% control over your reactions, and what you choose to entertain.*

Once again, this brings me to the culture of matching energy. You don't need to match energy to show that you are capable of "defending" yourself. When you do that, you are doing yourselves a disservice. You are no longer the one in power when you intentionally change your energy because of others. And they are now the ones who are in control of the energy that you put out. *If you must match energy, match positive energy.*

The Ultimate Self-Control

Self-control doesn't stop at controlling your actions and your words. It extends to your thoughts. Controlling your thoughts is the deepest form of self-control. Though your mind isn't a physical organ of the body, it shares similar characteristics. Meaning, the more you use it, the stronger it gets. Like a muscle, the more you practice specific ways of thinking, the more fluent and stronger your mind becomes at doing so.

When we train our minds to think a certain way, or block out negative influences, we become more equipped to control everything that comes after. Which are our feelings, words, actions, and perception. Keep in mind that, controlling our thoughts isn't the same as forcing ourselves into being in denial. In other words, ultimate self-control isn't the same as implementing toxic positivity.

Controlling Your Emotions Involves:

1. Acknowledging your feelings
2. Processing your feelings
3. Finding a way to appropriately express your feelings
4. Coming up with solutions for the situation at hand

5. Engaging in things that will keep you away from letting your mind run wild

4.B Reputation

Your reputation is the opinions and beliefs that others have of you. Needless to say that you can have a great reputation with someone, while having a terrible reputation with another. In a previous section, I've discussed how people's opinions of others are influenced by their own experiences, biases, and knowledge. However, a certain type of behavior from you is usually involved. Take a moment to think. What is your reputation in your community? Whether it's your church community, neighborhood, workplace, household, or school? If you believe that you have very different reputations in all of these communities. Take another moment to ask yourself a few self-check-in questions.

Self-Check-In Questions:

- Which opinion matters to you the most?
- Why does their opinion of you matter so much?
- Is this reputation a good or bad one?
- Why do you believe this reputation of you exist?
- Do you believe that this reputation is an accurate assumption of you?
- Does their opinion of you match the reputation that you have with yourself?
- If no, what is the reputation that you have with yourself?
- If the reputation that you have with yourself is a negative one, how can you change it?

People will always have an opinion about you, whether good or bad, accurate or inaccurate, and based on your past, present, or even your potentials. Sometimes, no matter how honest, trustworthy, accountable, respectful, graceful, or humble you are on a daily basis, there will always be a few people who will still think negatively about you. However, don't allow them to taint your perception of yourself. In your journey of self-transformation and healing, you are slowly building a great relationship and reputation with yourself, whether you realize it at first or not.

My desire for you is to have an amazing reputation with yourself. High sense of self-worth, self-love, and self-awareness all plays a part in how you form positive opinions about yourself. However, honesty and trustworthiness are the main contributing factors in your reputation. When you set goals or promises to yourself, make sure you do your best to keep to those promises. Whenever you set boundaries, be sure that you aren't allowing others to guilt-trip you into going against those boundaries. Sticking to your word highlights your trait of honesty, which is how you build trust and rapport with yourself. And solid trust has always been the key ingredient of a great reputation.

4.C Always Have A Plan

In order to progress in life, and find yourself achieving your goals and dreams, you have to show up for yourself daily.

Believe it or not, we set goals every day without realizing it. Whether it's to get up out of bed to make breakfast. Or, to get home at a certain time to watch a scheduled show. However, when you are setting more meaningful goals that will influence your future in some way, you have to become more strategic and intentional about how you create your plans. Make sure you aren't taking on more than you can handle, and that you are creating clear and realistic plans for your goals. When creating your plans, always keep in mind that overwhelming yourself with tasks will decrease the effectiveness of each goal.

A few affirmations when setting your goals and creating your plans are:

- There is room in this world for me and my dreams
- If I can think it, and create a sound plan to attain it, I can achieve it

<u>Meraki Note:</u> *Each achievement is a love letter to your younger self; telling him/her how grateful you are for the strength and resilience they've displayed in getting you to where you are today.*

In journal:

1. Write down some specific things you wish to achieve in the next 5 to 10 years
    a. You are welcome to change the years.
    b. For example 3-5 years, or 6 months to a year.
2. Use a highlighter to categorize your goals by colors
    a. The categories should represent the order you wish to achieve your goals
    b. For example, yellow may represents the goals you wish to achieve first, or in the next 5 months
3. Choose at most 3 goals to create a plan for
4. Follow Meraki Journey's Make It **P.L.A.I.N** Technique to construct a plan for each goal

When doing so, know that it's okay to be stubborn about your goals, but remember to be flexible about your methods. Sometimes your plan may fail, but keep in mind that this type of failure doesn't mean that your goal was a mistake. Nor does it mean that your goals are too big. All it means is that you may need to edit your **plan**.

When creating a plan remember to:

- ⇒ Never plan today without reference of yesterday.
  - o You are less likely to repeat the same mistakes of your past.
- ⇒ Never allow the worries of tomorrow to take away from the progress you can make today.
- ⇒ Never allow statistics to plan your life for you.
  - o Remember that all things are possible to those who belief, and work earnestly towards their goals.

It has been said that, when you live too much in the past, you are demonstrating regret, doubt, and ungratefulness for where you currently are in your life. This type of behavior is powerful enough to trigger various types of depression. However, I believe that you will experience similar affects when you live too much in the future. Yes, it's great to have goals, aspirations, and plans. However, you are putting yourself in jeopardy of neglecting your present self. You are also demonstrating ungratefulness for where you currently are in your life. When you do this, you will miss opportunities to appreciate your growth.

<u>Meraki Note:</u> *I encourage you to practice having a healthy balance in everything that you do. Learn from your past mistakes, appreciate where you are in life, and create attainable goals that make sense to who you desire to be.*

My Why
By: Taariq D. Jones

I've always been a goal-oriented person. Since I was a kid, I enjoyed things like reading a certain number of books in each year. In the second grade, I achieved my goal of reading 100 books, which made me extremely proud. I realized that I could achieve anything that I put my mind to. Once I was a little older, I set a goal to earn an athletic scholarship for Track—which I successfully did. Now, more recently my goal is to develop an asset that I can pass down to my kids. Although I had this goal, I didn't always know that I wanted to be in business. But I did always know how I wanted my life to be. And although I didn't have set plans as yet, I think my goals has guided me, and influenced most of my decisions throughout life.

There's plenty of things you can be in life, but what's the point if you're not living the life you dreamed of living? So for me, developing a business asset for myself will not only provide money—which I certainly love, but it also allows me more free time. This is important to me because time is something none of us can get back. I strongly believe that it's not always about what you're doing, but *why* you're doing it.

With my free time, I can spend my mornings working out as long as I want, eat a big breakfast, and spend quality time with my future wife as much as we'd like. Also, with the extra time and money, not only can I learn Japanese, but I can take a flight to Japan, attend Comic-Con, speak Japanese, and watch exclusive anime episodes, all while eating delicacies I've never tried before. I used to think this was dumb, but I meet too many people who "just want to have a *good* job". You should want the *best* for yourself. Best and good are two different things. So, see yourself in the best version you can be. And that includes *everything* in your dream lifestyle.

How many of you actually see yourself living your dreams? How many of you see yourself settling for what's in front of you, because dreams seem to never come true? How many of you are currently living a life that will move you towards your dream lifestyle? If not, know that you have the power to change anything that hinders you from achieving your goals. If you are thinking of starting a business, let this be your fuel to get you started, and your light when darkness is around you. Remember that it all starts with you, and you are enough!

The mechanics are simple:

1. Write your goals to make them real, and out of your head.
2. Find a mentor or a teacher who have certain habits that you can learn from
   a. Choose a mentor or teacher who is living a life that <u>inspires</u> your goals and plans
   b. Keep in mind that living from example isn't the same as trying to duplicate, or imitate someone else's life
3. Most importantly, be grateful and patience with yourself.

<u>**Self-Help Tip:**</u> A good home cooked meal isn't a 2-minute microwave tv dinner. It's chicken, Mac n cheese, collard greens, Turkey wings, jerk chicken, rice n peas, and the list goes on. These dishes take time, and shouldn't rushed. So, why try and rush yourself? Move with urgency, but be patience and take your time. Know that you can learn as you go. And anything you want to be, you just have to be willing to change or adjust a few things.

-Taariq D. Jones

Make It P.L.A.I.N.

When creating plans that aligns with your personal goals, it should not include others, such as lovers, family members, friends, or acquaintances. Your personal goals are about you and your development.

Meraki Journey's P.L.A.I.N. Technique:

- ◊ **Progress:** Take some alone time to think about which areas of your life need some progress or improvement.
    - You may document whatever comes to mind.
- ◊ **Limit:** Purposefully limit yourself to focus on 2 or 3 goals at a time
    - Don't overwhelm yourself by focusing on all of your goals at once.
- ◊ **Alignment:** In setting your goals, make sure it aligns with the person you are working towards becoming.
    - For example, if your desire is to become a fashion designer, the initial plan shouldn't be to buy a brand-new car—to fit an image or narrative.
    - Your plan should be to set up an L.L.C. or register your business name.
    - Alignment leads to intentionality.
- ◊ **Intentionality:** Be intentional with your plans.
    - Be strategic
    - Be clear
    - Be realistic
- ◊ **Necessary:** Make sure that your plans and methods are necessary for the journey.
    - Don't add unnecessary tasks that may distract or derail you from your journey

4.D Celebrate Your Achievements—Big And Small

Don't be the type of person who feels like nothing is ever good enough. Or that your progress isn't significant enough to be celebrated. Find joy in the progress that you are making each day, and always be grateful for life.

Remember to pace yourself in this beautiful marathon, and celebrate where you are in life. Don't be too hard on yourself by pushing yourself to move on to the next level, or the next best thing. I urge you to stop for a moment, and appreciate how far you have come. Appreciate who you could have been, but fought hard not to be. Appreciate what you have, even as you strive for more. And appreciate the people who stayed with you when others faded out of your life. When you appreciate these things, you are inspiring yourself to find ways to maximize all that you have. And you become resourceful, and efficient in using what you have.

With every minute that you spend making the most of your experiences, it will affect how you plan for the next stage of your life. Each new plan should begin with a celebration of all big and small achievements gained through your previous plan. Many of us will never hesitate to congratulate and celebrate others. But shy away from doing the same for ourselves. At times we may find ourselves downplaying our own achievements in order to avoid being perceived as boastful or bragging. *There's a difference between humility and downplaying something that you should very much be proud of.*

This is another reason why it is very important to surround yourself with those who are genuinely proud of your successes and accomplishments. People who are not intimidated by others' successes, and who are also making their own achievements. This way, you won't feel like you have to shy away from celebrating your wins. Never forget that you deserve to be proud of yourself! Despite if you are where you want to be in life or not. Don't wait until you've reached your goal to be proud of yourself. Be proud of yourself for each step that you take towards achieving each goal. By celebrating yourself, you are gifting yourself with **positive reinforcements**.

<u>**Meraki Note:**</u> *The positive reinforcement theory was introduced to us as from the moment we were born.*
- *When a child takes their first step, there is an outburst of cheers from parents and loved ones, in celebration. This type of reaction will encourage the child to continue to make progress.*
- *When a child has been good in school for a series of days, the teacher may put a gold star by their name. This reaction will encourage the child to continue to keep up the good work. It will also inspire their classmates to continue, or start behaving good as well.*
- *Throughout our adulthood, we also experience positive reinforcements by earning a paycheck weekly or bi-weekly, receiving raises or a promotion at work, or seeing the results of working out consistently. These types of rewards can be seen as positive reinforcements to persuade adults to continue their efforts.*

Acknowledgment and celebration of your achievements—whether big or small will give you the validation and reinforcement you need in order to keep that fire for success burning fiercely.

Regular Check-Ins With Self

Spiritual, physical, mental, emotional self-check-ins

When you don't make it a habit to self-check-in regularly, you may put yourself in jeopardy of falling back into old habits. If you tend to struggle with remembering to check in on yourself, you can make a schedule, or set alarms to check-in weekly. Remember that it's okay to have a routine in order to train yourself to become consistent.

Self-check-ins are all about maintenance. When the maintenance person of any entity does their routine visit, there's a chance that they won't find anything wrong with the place. However, if they do find that there's something deteriorating or isn't working anymore, they are required to make some changes, or bring it to the owner's attention. They wouldn't just take note of the situation, and leave it to worsen over time. This is the same concept of self-maintenance A.K.A self-check-ins.

When self-checking-in, if you realize that something that used to work for you, is no longer working, you are responsible to make the appropriate changes. If a personality trait isn't working out for you in a situation, you may need to adjust some things. If you feel like a relationship is no longer working, or is causing negative ripples in your life, you may need to remove that person from your life, or adjust the way you interact with them. Whether you change the role that they play in your life, or the level of access that they may have to you. Also, if you find that your job is no longer aligning with who you are, where you are in life, or where desire to elevate to, you may need to make some healthy changes.

Meraki Note: *Don't allow the fear of change, or your comfortability to cause you to turn a blind eye on what you discover when you have self-checked-in.*

Our Why: Our reasons for consistent self-check-ins are similar to why we should always practice a healthy balance, when creating plans for our goals. Regular self-check-ins are essential to keep yourself in the present. A lot of times we may get stuck in the past. Especially when we haven't fully healed from things, or when we are fixated on things that we regret about our past. Other times we may focus too much on the future; by always planning ahead, or striving for the next best things. In both scenarios, we are not allowing ourselves to be present.

Meraki Note: *Don't neglect who you are today by focusing on the next best thing. Who you are in this moment needs your attention, praise, grace, and nurture for you to be your best self in the near future. Continue to remain proud of the progress you're making, no matter how small.*

Regular self-check-ins are also essential in order to know when to take wellness breaks, ask for help, set better boundaries, reevaluate our self-care journey, and putting ourselves in check when needed. As our journey unfolds, we are bound to become wiser and more sensitive to negative behaviors—even if it's our own negative behaviors. This is why self-checking-in is the perfect way to initiate self-reflection. During self-reflection, it's okay to say things like, "What I said earlier to that cashier was wrong and insensitive." Or "I know my feelings are valid, but that didn't give me the right to speak to my friend that way."

Meraki Note: *If you feel that you could have done better, train yourself to do better. And if an apology is warranted, pride yourself on issuing a sincere apology to who you've offended. Even if that person is yourself.*

How to self-check-in?

Start off by creating a schedule to checking in on yourself weekly, until it becomes a habit.

<u>*Routine*</u> → <u>**Consistency**</u>

Self-Check-In Questions:

Self-check-ins can happen anywhere. While driving, in the shower, cooking, or meditating.

- Am I doing okay today?
- What is taking up my mind lately?
- How am I feeling today?
- What kind of energy have I been giving off lately?
- How do I feel about my job?
- Is the argument that I had yesterday affecting my mood today?
- Am I avoiding any necessary emotions?
- What have I been feeding my mind, spirit, and body lately?
- How am I feeling about my life overall?
- How are my relationships doing?

Meraki Note: *Setting goals, acknowledging your accomplishments, changing or transforming your liabilities, adjusting boundaries, and setting standards all starts with self-check-ins and self-reflection.*

Conclusion

Throughout Meraki Journey, many of the topics catered to the increasing of good hormones in your body. These hormones are known as dopamine, oxytocin, serotonin, and endorphin. To remember these hormones, we will use the acronym **DOSE**. When we engage in certain activities, our body send a signal to our brain, which causes us to feel loved, pleasured, or happy.

Dopamine: *The reward hormones*
Topics like: **Positive Reinforcement**
Activities: *Self-care, completing a task, shopping, eating good food, celebrating wins, and getting enough sleep*
**This hormone helps with decision-making

Oxytocin: *The love or trust hormones*
Topics like: **Choose your company wisely**
Activities: *Deep conversations, intimate connections, giving and receiving compliments*
**This hormone helps with managing genuine friendship

Serotonin: *The happy hormones*
Topics like: **Sacred spaces and peace**
Activities: *Listening to music, mediating, eating healthy, walking in nature, writing or journaling, and sun exposure*
**This hormone helps with "having a good day"

Endorphin: *The pain or stress reliever hormones*
Topics like: **What you feed your mind spirit and body**
Activities: *Laughing, exercise, eating chocolate and/or spicy foods, relaxing, and physical touch*
**This hormone helps with feeling relaxed and calm

Remember that it's the small habits that will affect your life the most, and sometimes in small increments. It's how you start your day each morning. It's how you speak to yourself and others throughout the day, no matter what. It's the people you choose to spend your time with. It's who and what has access to you. It's who and what you choose to invest your energy into. And it's what you feed your mind, spirit, and body. All of which makes up who you are. So, consume content that reflects the life you envision for yourself, and surround yourself with people whose life reflects your life goals and morals.

Some will commend you, support you, celebrate you, and even decide to start their own self-transformational journey, because your journey has inspired them. However, some will try to guilt-trip you by trying to make you feel that you have neglected or abandoned them. So, please pay attention. The ones who aren't happy about your new journey, are most likely the ones who have been benefiting from your negative behaviors and lack of boundaries. I encourage you to stay the course. Don't worry about what others think of you. Be concern about what you think of yourself.

This entire journey surrounds the core of truly getting to know who you are in a new light. Become clear about the person you want to become, and what you want to achieve in this life. On the journey of getting to know yourself—as much as you can, try to give yourself the luxury of surrounding yourself with things that excites you, relaxes you, and inspires you. In addition to surrounding yourself with people who motivate, challenge, celebrate, and empowers you. Lastly, when setting clear and realistic goals, always remember to make it P.L.A.I.N.; and make sure that you are creating a paper trail for you to look back, and see all the progress you have been making.

HEALING & SELF-TRANSFORMATION

I hope that beautiful things happen to you. And when they do, I hope that you believe that you are worthy of every single one of them. Never forget that you are beautiful. You are smart. You are blessed. You are deserving of great and wonderful things. You are seen. And, yes, you are loved. I am proud of you. I am rooting for you. And I am grateful for you. I pray for God's blessings of abundance, fruitfulness, and multiplication to remain a part of your inheritance now and forevermore.

Dear GOD

By: Jesmine Shelton

    What a mighty God you are. We worship you for not what you've done but just simply for who you are! GOD thank you for loving us continuously even when we fall short of loving ourselves. God, I thank you for loaning me such a great support system. It takes a village & I'm beyond grateful of you for mine. God thank you for shifting my mind & preparing me to fulfill my purpose. Use me GOD for the rest of my days because I'm not me without you. Nothing in this world amounts to you, and I know that with you nothing in this world will ever lead me stray. Strengthen our faith so no matter what we face we rely solely on you. God, I thank you for pouring blessings on my union. Use them as well because, I don't want to be alone when it's time to take my seat at the table GOD. I pray you remove anything and anyone who appears to represent you but puts in overtime for the devil. Keep us bulletproof cause we are in a time where killing & rioting is at an all-time high. Every time we make it home safe with our loved ones it's only one who we think of "Father God" Amen.

-Jesmine Shelton

AUTHOR'S MESSAGE

No more will we use the statement, "hurting people, hurt people". Instead we will say, "<u>unhealed people hurt people</u>". Because no matter how badly hurt we have been, once we are healed, matured, and learned from our past pain, our desire will be to see others healed as well.

Let's break free from the social norms. Let's try to treat others the way that we want to be treated. And let's learn to give each other some grace, as we all do our best to maneuver through this complex experience that we call <u>life</u>.

We are all unique individuals. So, it's safe to say that we all may not find peace and healing the same way, nor at the same pace. Be patient with one another, and know that there's no *best* way to achieve healing and self-transformation.

Life is so much more than the simplicities of black and white, right and wrong, beautiful and ugly. Life is truly better defined as a multilevel, multifaceted journey. So, enjoy every twist and turn, ups and downs, and accomplishments and lesson learned.

All the best,

Dr. Christina Baker

Made in the USA
Middletown, DE
16 February 2025

71078999R00075